Tom Molineaux: From bondage to baddest man on the planet

By Bill Calogero

JC Publications
Sacramento, Ca.

Tom Molineaux: From bondage to baddest man on the planet

Bill Calogero

(ISBN-13): 978-0-692-48410-4

Cover design by Elderlemon Designs

Manufactured in the United States of America

JC Publications
Sacramento, Ca
JCPublication.com

This book is dedicated to the life of Tom Molineaux; a man who was born a slave, fought for his freedom, became the first American heavyweight champion and found riches and fame far more than he thought was ever possible.

I will continue the fight.

Table of Contents

Acknowledgements

So much went into the writing of this book that it's extremely hard to acknowledge everything that made it possible. From the people who have supported me and my journey in the sport of boxing and the ones who have believed in me and this project, to the people who have not and went as far as saying "stop chasing your dreams" because all of them assisted in creating the drive and or the fuel I needed to get it done. Fortunately, due to the combination of support and negativity, I was able to move forward and continue, although at times I needed to slap myself to make it to the end. Now I can finally say WE made it!

I say we because I feel that this book could NOT have been possible at all if it weren't for the following people. I hope I have not forgotten anyone, and if I have, I am truly sorry. It was certainly not intentional.

Special Thanks

First and foremost, must go to Daxx Khan for all of the work he does for me and the BillyCBoxing brand, which includes our daily boxing talk program, the Talkin Boxing With Billy C TV & Radio Show, the www.BillyCBoxing.com website, BillyCBoxing Blog and our many social media accounts, all on a daily basis. (Trust me Daxx, your dedication, hard work and loyalty does not go unnoticed!) Without Daxx Khan, I would have never had the time to even think about doing this book.

Alex Pierpaoli who put in countless hours assisting me in the nuts & bolts of this book by proofreading each chapter and spending the extra time in suggesting the proper wording   and or edits to make this book possible. Alex means a lot to me and has for a very long time….Thanks my man!

Clay Moyle who was one of the first people to not only help me find resources for the research I needed to do for this book through his own personal boxing book collection and his www.Prizefightingbooks.com inventory, he also spent countless time in making and providing me my own copies, which made my work much easier to do. Without Clay, there is no Tom Molineaux book.

David Bergin for providing all of the photos and or sketches used in this book, which he has spent years finding and collecting for his Vintage Boxing and other Sports Memorabilia company.

And finally, a Very Special thanks goes to James Curl and JC Publications for having the faith in me and this book to work as hard as he did in order to publish it and make it available to anyone, anywhere. Thank you Jim!

I must also thank all of the following people and or websites for their help and assistance in making this book possible: Scotty Crouse, Larry Hazzard, Colleen Aycock, Mark Scott, Patrick Myler, Bill Paxton, Scott Noble, Austin Killeen, Coach K, Emily Harney, www.Pugilistica.com, Jack Cawley, Lindsey Williams, all of the IBRO members, www.BoxingTreasures.com, Sal "Rocky" Cenicola, John Moceyunas & the entire crew from LDLTV and www.YouTube.com/TalkinBoxing.

I must also thank and give credit to all of my personal favorite All-Time-Great fighters (in no particular order) that helped make the sport of boxing what it is today by seeking out the most difficult challenges to prove they were not just ordinary fighters, but they were the best of their era and wanted to prove it for more reasons than just money and in my opinion, should never be forgotten:

Sugar Ray Robinson, Jack Johnson, Sonny Liston, Jack Dempsey, Mike Tyson, Marvin Hagler, Tommy Hearns, Sam Langford, Ray "Boom-Boom" Mancini, Joe Louis, Sugar Ray Leonard, Rocky Marciano, Billy Costello, Muhammad Ali, Barney Ross, Ernie Shavers, Marlon Starling, Benny Leonard, Charley Burley, Bernard Hopkins, Manny Pacquiao, Henry Armstrong, Harry Greb, Roberto Duran, Jersey Joe Walcott, Joe Gans, Barney Ross, Mickey Walker, Stanley Ketchel, Archie Moore, Ezzard Charles, Carmen Basilo, Julio Cesar Chavez, Oscar De La Hoya, Mickey Walker, Roy Jones Jr., James Toney, Jack Britton, Willie Pep, Ron Lyle, and Billy Conn. (I could go on and on, but I have to stop sometime!)

I also want to thank all of the viewers, listeners and followers of the Talkin Boxing With Billy C TV & Radio Program because without them, the sport of boxing would not be the same for me.

And finally, I would like to thank the listener who had emailed me after hearing me talk about Tom Molineaux and how he was robbed of the world title in December of 1810 during the Talkin Boxing With Billy C TV & Radio program asking where he could find the YouTube video of the fight.

I admit I didn't know much about Tom Molineaux before I read Bill Calogero's book. In fact, I was fairly ignorant of anything prior to John L. Sullivan, pugilistically speaking.

There was a vast field of buried treasure that I unwittingly passed over again and again.

Thankfully, Calogero has unearthed one of those missing gems in the story of Tom Molineaux—an American slave who, remarkably, won his freedom with his fists and used those fists to achieve unprecedented success and celebrity status in early 19th-century England. However, as fact is not only stranger than fiction but often more tragic, so Molineaux's story does not end happily. His is a rags-to-riches-to-rags story that would seem unbelievable even by Hollywood's standards. Molineaux's rise from slave to celebrity is as uplifting as his downfall and ultimate demise are unsettling, sort of Charles Dickens meets William Shakespeare, or *Rocky* meets *Leaving Las Vegas*. To his credit, Calogero pulls no punches and tells Molineaux's story in all its exultant, yet bitter reality.

With neither patronizing adoration nor sanctimonious disapproval, he gives us Tom Molineaux's life the way it was--the good, the bad, and the tragic. In so doing he leaves the reader with a perplexing, yet thought-provoking sociological dilemma. Is Molineaux an inspirational hero to be admired or ill-fated anti-hero to be pitied? Does he represent the best of what's in man, what man can achieve regardless of circumstance or social status? Or, does he represent man at his worst, the failures human beings are seemingly bound to make when they find success and embrace the celebrity life they so passionately obsess over? Or maybe he's simply a reflection of the strengths and weaknesses that comprise us all, a fusion of both fortitude and fragility which not only comprises but makes us human.

Whatever the reader decides regarding Molineaux the *man*, Calogero leaves no doubt what to do with Molineaux the *fighter*. In this he is dogmatic and unequivocal: Molineaux was not only the first black boxing champion in this country's history, but the very first American champion, regardless of race, a fact many have overlooked and an oversight Calogero passionately and scrupulously seeks to correct. He takes the reader through meticulous detail of Molineaux's boxing career and greatest fights, the climax being Molineaux's classic title fight with English champion, Tom Cribb, toward which the book builds from early on. Here is where Calogero is at his best, providing his readers with a fascinating round-by-round description of the fight with such accuracy and clarity one can easily envision the raucous crowd, feel the dampness of the frigid weather, see the blood and mud on the fighters' bodies, hear the sounds of fist meeting flesh and bone, and sense the tension and drama of an epic struggle which stretched two men's wills and ability to absorb punishment beyond human comprehension.

Whatever one gets out of reading this book, Molineaux's fight with Cribb (along with the equally grueling and just as detailed rematch) will be unforgettable. My guess is, though, that like me the reader will find Molineaux's entire story not too quickly forgotten. It's a familiar storyline with relatively unfamiliar characters Calogero has refreshingly rediscovered for the boxing fan and beyond. I'm grateful to Calogero for sharing this previously overlooked treasure with me, and after reading this book you will be too.

Scott "Scotty" Crouse
Boxing Radio Personality & Historian

The sport of boxing has a long and illustrious history, one that is filled with stories of men born in poverty who rose to prominence and financial riches beyond their imagination as a result of their skill with their fists. But for every one of those Cinderella type stories there are hundreds that ended tragically, with the fighter physically impaired, penniless, or with little, if any, lasting legacy in their chosen field of endeavor.

The story of Tom Molineaux is as tragic as they get, and Bill Calogero, the popular and entertaining host of the Talkin Boxing TV & Radio Shows has come forward and filled a longtime void with this book. Bill has spent years researching and writing this story and it was a daunting task given the fact that the records of most of his fights in the United States were not preserved and there is so little information available about much of Tom's career. Despite those obstacles, Bill has done a remarkable job, and I'm confident that the story's readers will discover that it's every bit as informative and entertaining as Bill's show is.

Born a slave on a plantation in Richmond, Virginia in 1784, Molineaux's childhood, as it was for so many other young men born in servitude, was one of long hours of hard labor and physical abuse. Maybe it was partly a function of all that hard work that he developed into such a tremendous physical specimen with large broad shoulders, a deep chest, and a thick neck by the time he was 17 years old. Regardless of how his marvelous physique came about, it created an opportunity for Tom to win his personal freedom in a contest against another slave, and sent him down a path where he became a professional bare knuckle fighter that should have become one of the best known success stories in the history of the sport.

It's difficult to comprehend just how difficult the road that Tom travelled to fight for a world title must have been in   that period of time. Imagine for a moment what the odds must have been against him achieving his freedom in the first place. And then, how unlikely it would have been for him to not only succeed over the next few years as a professional fighter in New York City, where slavery wasn't outlawed until 1827, but to such a degree that he became recognized by many as America's bare knuckle champion. Then, to top it off, he travels to England, and by all rights, not only defeated a man who is now generally acknowledged as the sports first world champion, but knocked him unconscious. Well, as I said already, Molineaux's story should have gone down in history as boxing's greatest Cinderella story ever.

The fact that Molineaux is not celebrated as America's first world heavyweight boxing champion, let alone the first black heavyweight boxing champion of the world, almost a century before Jack Johnson received acclaim for the latter, can only be attributed to the racial climate of the time, and is surely the greatest example of injustice ever incurred by a participant in a world championship contest.

My good friend Bill Calogero will fill you in on the details of that particular battle with England's champion, and why it was such a great miscarriage of justice. You will also learn about the events that shaped Tom's life, all the other important contests in his career, and finally what became of this largely forgotten and important figure in boxing's history. Bill does a wonderful job of telling Molineaux's story and recapturing the lost legacy of the man who was truly America's first world heavyweight boxing champion.

Clay Moyle
Boxing Author & Historian

Foreword

I guess I first met *Billy C* at the fights.

Bill Calogero, the author of this book, and boxing personality Billy C are the same guy and I met the two of them, unsurprisingly, while sitting ringside, watching live boxing. It was there at Mohegan Sun, watching Devon Alexander knock out Juan Urango, where I enjoyed sharing observations throughout the night with this mustachioed Italian New Yorker and knew immediately I was seated beside someone who at his very core, was all fight-fan.

I also learned about Calogero's TV & radio show, ***Talkin' Boxing with Billy C***, which had more than 8 years on the air at that time, delivering two hours of boxing talk each episode, five days a week.

And after that night I became a subscriber and enjoyed e-mailing the show and having Billy C, Calogero's on-air alter ego, respond to my comments and questions. Billy C's show was just the thing for this boxing fan, a daily outlet of pure boxing talk that covered the entire sport from the big names to the little club shows. And although I didn't always agree with the issues he brought up, Billy C's broadcasts were always entertaining and full of rants against fighters who skirted challenges and cherry-picked opponents. Billy C would rail against promoters who don't promote, or he'd embarrass self-aggrandizing referees and overbearing television commentators. On his show Billy C was always railing against something. It made for great boxing entertainment and most of the time, he was right.

About three months after our encounter at ringside, I met Bill Calogero again in Canastota, NY, at the International Boxing Hall of Fame's induction weekend in June. Our shared admiration for boxing history had brought us together as writers in the same anthology by Colleen Aycock and Mark Scott, <u>The First Black Boxing Champions</u>, available for sale there at the induction sponsored collector's show. We stood together beside a table full of books for some time at that show, meeting our co-authors and schmoozing with boxing fans there in the sticky, crowded Canastota High School Gym. That weekend Calogero extended the generous offer to come on his radio program and talk about one of my favorite fighters, whom I had written about in the anthology, Sam McVey. A couple of weeks later in July of two thousand and ten, I called in to talk with Billy C about McVey on-the-air and have been calling-in just about every Wednesday since then to talk about more greats from boxing history. Calogero welcomed me into the Billy C Boxing family and each week I am thrilled to be able to help him with the Blast-From-the Past where together we discuss great fighters from yesteryear and their impact on the sport.

Since then, through my association with Calogero I've learned much more about boxing and boxing history, as well as broadcasting. Together we've even called fights from varied locales, including a baseball field in Jupiter, Florida, Lions Clubs, high school gyms and exposition halls in remote locations. Boxing, even small-time regional boxing, though often over-looked as a legitimate sport is surely not dead, and Bill Calogero is someone who has convinced me of that.

And perhaps most importantly I've also been convinced that boxing is a sport where there remain wrongs to be righted and untold stories that need to be shouted out and marked down. What you hold in your hands is Bill Calogero's effort to do exactly that.

These pages represent the most complete and accessible account of the life and battles of Tom Molineaux, a Virginia slave who won his freedom with his fists and bested the Bare-Knuckle Heavyweight Champion of the World. Calogero will introduce you to Molineaux, his opponents and his contemporaries, men who slammed fist against bone in the wild, outdoor, bare-knuckle bouts of England in the 18th century. Here you will learn of one of the first great American sports idols, a man who, but for the color of his skin, would be and should be immortalized by history. Calogero thoroughly documents the arc of Tom Molineaux's stardom, as it burns brightly and roars across the world of boxing before flaming-out, scorching a path too many great fighters will go on to repeat.

In the following pages, Billy C will give you something to rail against when you hear of the dastardly deeds done to this unsung American hero. With prose as plain and direct as a Molineaux hammer-fist to the clavicle, Bill Calogero will unravel and uncover some of the mysteries lost through time about one of boxing's pioneers. Like the passionate following Calogero showed me in the small regional fights we covered together, here he will connect you to the squared-circles of England in times gone by. And like his radio program feeds the needs of any modern fight-fan, this work and Molineaux's tale will do the same for people of all ages and any color.

While Billy C's outspokenness and passion will draw you into these pages, Bill Calogero's methodical accounting of what took place will convince you of Molineaux's greatness and impact on the sport. Those two sides of this author came together through the writing of this work, much the way a prize-fighter funnels aggression through control to find the perfect fight strategy. The sum of those efforts is what you are about to read. Bill Calogero is your man in charge.
Obey his commands and protect yourself at all times, for this is the true and tragic tale of Tom Molineaux.

Alex Pierpaoli – June 2015, Author, Historian & Boxing Personality

Tom Molineaux Intro

I first got interested in the Bare Knuckle Boxing Era when I began reading the Boxiana Series of books written by Pierce Egan. Egan is not only regarded as the first boxing reporter but most regard him as the very first onsite Sports Reporter. His Boxiana series gives us a History of boxing from the 1700's through the early 1800's in England.

While reading about these extremely tough men who fought with their bare knuckles during a time when many didn't survive long after the fights, win or lose, or even make it through the contest itself, I came across a fighter named Tom Molineaux.

Molineaux was an American who was born a slave. He left the United States a free man, having won his freedom in the ring, and traveled to England bringing the title of the American Heavyweight Champion with him. He had one goal; to seek out and defeat England's heavyweight champion, Tom Cribb. As I read Egan's ringside description of this great battle between Cribb and Molineaux, one line made an everlasting impression on me.

Considering that Molineaux was a black man, from the south, one would have to assume he was a very dark skinned black man and was described as such; "As black as Coal," "The Black" & "The Moor" where all used to describe him and the color of his skin. Cribb, on the other hand, was described as a very white Caucasian man: "Lilly White" and "White as Milk" were used to describe him and the color of his skin.

As I read Egan's account of the fight, he wrote that this contest was one of the most brutal he had ever witnessed to date and that the two men had inflicted much damage on e a c h other. He said that by the nineteenth round, both men were so disfigured and covered with blood, that you weren't able to distinguish them apart. Can you imagine that? How badly would two men have to have beaten each other in order to make a statement like that?

After reading Egan's description of this brutal affair, I had to know more about Molineaux. It was then I began researching Tom, which no easy task was considering that the United States has seemingly done a great job in shoving anything that had to do with Slavery under the carpet, and Slavery is where it all began for Tom Molineaux. After all, he fought his way to freedom as a form of entertainment for plantation owners, who would put Slave against Slave in fights that in most cases, ended in death. Add to that the fact no one seemed to care about the lives of Slaves during the time, resulted in little to no documentation of their accomplishments, or even demise.

When it was all said and done, my research took over seven years to uncover, what I feel, is everything possibly available on the man, Tom Molineaux.

I have been involved in the sport of boxing for well over thirty years as an amateur boxer, a manager, an adviser, a promoter, a matchmaker, a writer, a historian, a boxing gym owner, doing TV & webcast boxing commentary and the host of a daily boxing talk program, the Talkin Boxing With Billy C TV & Radio show.

In my opinion, based on one of the most well-known boxers to enter the ring in the past thirty years, Molineaux was "Mike Tyson" almost 200 years before Iron Mike was even born. Molineaux's story is a common one in the sport of boxing. Most of our past greats were born into poverty and used boxing as a way out and into a better life. Even that is topped by Molineaux, who was born as a slave and used boxing as a means to gain his freedom, better his life, travel the World, and become famous. But sadly, as is the case with many of our past, present and unfortunately, will be with our future fighters, Molineaux's story did not have a happy ending.

I think what bothers me the most about Tom is the fact that to me, this man, this American, didn't get his due during his life, and to this day, he STILL is not getting the credit he deserves. Even in the boxing World, he is not regarded as the first American Heavyweight Champion, in which he clearly w a s , as you will read and learn in this book. That honor wrongly is credited to a fighter that fought nearly five decades after Molineaux's death. To make matters worse, Molineaux isn't even regarded as the first black American Heavyweight Champion, in which those honors go to a man who fought almost seventy years after the death of Tom Molineaux.

The sad truth is, it was and still is, due to the color of his skin. Add to that the fact that he was born during slavery, as a slave, in my opinion, the United States has tried and continues to try and keep hidden away from us today and all future generations anything that points to that horrific time during its history. Slavery is an unforgivable blemish for the United States of America, but it's still fact and it IS part of the history of the "land of the free and home of the brave." Tom Molineaux lived in the land of the free, during a time when HE was not, but as you will see, the man was very brave.

One simple fact points to this and it's there for everyone to see. When Molineaux fought Tom Cribb on that cold and rainy day in December of 1810, it was billed as the first World Heavyweight Contest. Why? Because Tom Cribb held the Heavyweight title of England and Tom Molineaux held the Heavyweight Title of America. How else could it have been billed that way? If Molineaux was not considered the Heavyweight Champion of America, then the fight would have been billed as the Championship of England. It was not. Tom Cribb is credited as being the First World Heavyweight

Champion when he beat (and even that was a huge debate which you will read in this book) Tom Molineaux. The only way he accomplished that (or did he?) was to beat the American Heavyweight Champion. Why doesn't history give Molineaux the credit he deserves? Was it because he was born black and as a Slave on a Virginia plantation?

You can judge that for yourself.

Tom was not only a great fighter and part of boxing history; he was an American and was a very important part of American History. It's in my opinion that we must finally give this man the credit he deserves. He should have been able to get this long overdue credit during his lifetime. We failed there. The least we can do is give it to him now. For once, instead of shoveling wrong-doings under the carpet, we must correct a wrong and make it right. We owe that to Tom.

I hope you enjoy this book as much as I enjoyed writing it and more importantly, as much as I enjoyed learning about Tom Molineaux.

Bill Calogero

Chapter 1

The sport of boxing, in one form or another, has been around for more than a thousand years.

Today's version of Professional Boxing began its evolution in England during the 1700s. Jack Broughton, considered the "Father of Boxing," combined the sport of Fencing and fighting and the term Prizefighting was born. Prizefighting was very popular in England, despite being illegal. As the sport evolved, the art of hitting an opponent but avoiding being hit at the same time began to be regarded as the "Sweet Science" As the techniques of hitting and not getting hit progressed, Prizefighting began to take shape and the fighters in England were considered the world's best. The contests had rules, were well organized and promoted and they generally drew large crowds. The rules were simple. No gloves were used. A round ended when one of the two combatants hit the ground. Once the round was over, you had thirty-seconds to come out for the next round. If you could not, you lost. You couldn't gouge at your opponents eyes and you couldn't hit a man while he was down. Aside from that, anything else was legal.

Boxing soon found its way to America, but the style of boxing there was very different than what was going on in England. The fighting itself was void of "The Science" of boxing. There were no rules and for the most part, fighting was a quick way to resolve a dispute between two men (or women), often happening with little notice or pre-planning. It was looked down upon and very little press was given to it with the exception of accounts from the participants and spectators of these brutal contests.

There is no doubt that while prizefighting had become very popular in England during the mid 1700s, some bouts were taking place in America in one form another. During this time a country was just being conceived and the talk in the American Colonies was of revolution and liberation, not of sport. Life in America was not easy. In addition to finding its way politically, it was a daily struggle to live in a very rapidly changing world. Slaves performed the majority of the physical labor in the farming industries. Slave trading in its self was a big business. During this time, many owners of the bigger plantations in the South used slaves to perform the daily workload. Slave traders would buy, sell and trade slaves the same way you would buy, sell or trade a horse, however in a lot of cases, the slaves were treated far worse than the horses.

Zachary Molineaux was a Virginia slave. It's not known whether a slave trader transported him from the African continent or if he was born into slavery in America. We do know that during the American Revolution he fought for the Colonies and helped win their freedom. Whether he was forced to fight with his owner, or whether he joined on his own, he fought valiantly for America and was considered a hero. After the war, he was returned to the Molineaux plantation in Virginia to continue his life in bondage. How and where he learned the Sweet Science is unknown, but it's most probable that he picked it up during his military service. According to Nat Fleischer, there was an article written in 1788 in a Philadelphia newspaper that indicated a Mr. Silas Freeman brought Zachary Molineaux up on assault charges. The article said, *"Zachary Molineaux, who fought for the Colonists in the recent strife with England, was hailed before our Magistrate last Friday to answer the charge of assault, brought against him by Silas Freeman. Molineaux, whose record of loyalty did him well at the hearing, was admonished and dismissed after an apology. This war hero who is a conquering pugilist and retired undefeated, promised never again commit an assault."*

Nat Fleischer, "The Ring" magazine's founder, credited Zachary Molineaux as the man responsible for bringing Bare Knuckle Boxing to the United States in his book titled *Black Dynamite*. Zachary had five sons, Elizah, Ebenezer, Franklin, Moses and Tom. He lived the remainder of his life as a slave on the Molineaux Plantation and died sometime around 1798.

Zachary's son, Tom Molineaux was born a slave on March 23, 1784 in Richmond, Virginia on the Molineaux Plantation. Just as his father had done before him, Tom took on the Molineaux surname as he belonged to the Molineaux family, considered one of the "First Families of Virginia." That meant they were descendants of one of the English aristocratic houses to whom King Charles had granted lands on an extensive scale in the New World.

Although records are scarce, it's likely Tom's childhood was similar to that of other children born into slavery during this era. It consisted of working long hard days in the fields of the plantation. As was the custom, a young male slave began working side-by- side with the adult men by the time he was nine or ten. This type of work made the boys very strong. By the time Tom was 14 years old, his father had died and young Tom solidified his position around the plantation as a chief handyman. He had big, broad shoulders, a deep chest and a thick neck. His appearance showed that he was a very strong and powerful young man. He soon became the constant companion of young Algernon Molineaux, who was the son of the Plantation's owner.

Algernon was a reckless, dissipated youth who enjoyed the vices of the English aristocracy of the time. He was particularly fond of sports and Prize-

Fighting was his favorite. Algernon often attended events where the slaves were put against each other and would fight for the amusement of their masters. Frequently, the masters had very high stakes placed upon the result.

Slave fighting was a well-organized fight card that would usually pit slaves from one plantation against slaves from another for the purpose of entertainment, as well as the possibility of financial gain through gambling. Some argue that these encounters did not take place at all because it did not make sense for a slave owner to put his best worker in such a compromising position, risking injury and even death for the sake of entertainment. However, these matches not only gave Plantation owners and their family and guests "something to do" on a Friday or Saturday evening, the money one could make from gambling on the matches could replace a slave virtually overnight. Slave fighting was not something that took place often, but when it did, because it usually was presented as plantation vs. plantation, or family vs. family, in addition to the substantial financial gain, pride was definitely at stake as well.

In 1801, when Tom was 17, Randolph Peyton, the owner of a neighboring Plantation, threw a party. During the party, Peyton boasted that there wasn't a slave in any of Virginia's Plantation families that could beat his slave, Abe in a bare-knuckle contest. Algernon was at the party. He had been enjoying himself to the max that night and felt confident that Tom could beat Abe. There was no doubt that Algernon was quite intoxicated at the time, but he was so sure that "his" Tom would come out the victor versus Abe, he accepted the challenge and officially nominated Tom. Stakes were posted and bets were made, and in the morning after the party, when he came to his senses, Algernon was rather shocked to find that he stood to lose no less than a hundred thousand dollars! Even though he was wealthy, this kind of money was way out of his reach. To make matters worse, his father would   never have approved of such business. But it was too late to change things at that point so he had no choice but to risk his family's entire estate on the outcome of this fight. The fight was scheduled in two months and Algernon figured that gave him plenty of time to see that Tom could be properly trained and, would assure victory for the Molineaux Estate. From this point, his only business was Tom.

Algernon knew he needed the help of someone who was practiced in the finer art of prizefighting; more than what was the norm in the United States during the time. As luck would have it, there was such a man in town with the reputation of knowing the "Sweet Science." His name was Patrick Davis. Davis was a sailor for England on the ship Margaret Elizabeth. He was in town as his ship was preparing for its next voyage. Algernon immediately sent word to Davis and hired him to help train Tom. Now, Algernon felt things were in place to secure not only Tom's victory in the ring but also the Molineaux Estate.

But after working with Tom for a little while, Davis told Algernon that he thought Tom was too docile and was not taking his training seriously. When learning of this, Algernon became furious. Although the Molineaux family was known to be "kind to their slaves" Tom was beaten. When Davis and Tom resumed training, Tom had become even less interested in learning the manly-art of prizefighting. When Algernon again checked on Tom's status, Davis told him that things looked bleak if Tom did not learn more and learn faster. Feeling the pressure of what was at stake; Algernon said he would beat Tom again, this time "even worse." But Davis thought of another approach. He suggested that Tom not be beaten, and instead, be offered his freedom and $100 in the event he won the match. Should he lose, the Molineaux family would be bankrupt and the fate of all of its slaves would be unknown anyway. Algernon agreed and made the offer to Tom. At the thought of gaining his freedom, Tom's attitude changed completely. He began training very hard and became a good student for Davis. When Algernon went to Davis for a report, Davis was pleased to inform the young master that Tom was doing very well. They continued to train and train hard. By the time Tom was getting the most out of training camp, six weeks had gone by and it was time for the fight.

On fight night, the atmosphere was like the "Super Bowl" or "World Series." There were people in attendance that traveled from as far as one hundred fifty miles away that consisted of both the sporting and non-sporting type. They came by horse, carriage and on foot. In addition to the spectators' general feeling of anticipation of the upcoming battle, at least one entire estate was at stake, as was a man's freedom. Tom entered the ring in top shape, as did Abe. Once the fight started, Tom controlled the action, giving Abe a brutal beating and winning the contest, pounding Abe into submission in less than five bloody rounds. Everyone in attendance was treated to an entertaining display of prizefighting in its most brutal and barbaric form. The term "Sweet Science" could hardly be associated with this contest but everyone who witnessed the event, enjoyed themselves, especially Tom's young master, Algernon. True to his word, Algernon granted Tom his freedom and because the brash young master made out so well financially on Tom's great victory, Algernon gave Tom $500 instead of the $100 he promised! Tom didn't waste any time. He took nothing but the clothes on his back, his money and his newfound Freedom, and left the Virginia Plantation where he was born for good.

Some say that Patrick Davis traveled with Tom after the fight in Virginia. Many also feel that Davis should be considered one of the first boxing managers and or advisors; because of the shrewd negotiations he performed to help aid in the success of the fight as well as the training of Tom Molineaux. Without Patrick Davis, the fight may not have had the same outcome. Unfortunately, the whereabouts of Davis immediately following the Molineaux-Peyton bout in Virginia during 1801 have been lost. Some say he returned to the sea life and eventually returned to England to live out his days. Others say he was lost at sea. The truth is, from the day Tom Molineaux was granted his freedom, there is no record of further contact made between the two men and no other information that can be backed up about Patrick Davis.

Chapter 2

It's not known exactly how he got there, or where he may have stopped along the way, or even the exact date in which he arrived, but by 1804, Molineaux was in New York making his living as a professional fighter. He ended up in the Catherine Street Market area, where black men could fight each other and occasionally fight the English Sailors that were on shore leave. The Catherine Slip during this time was one of the busiest ports in New York and was filled with a motley mix of fighters, seamen, street performers, businessmen and lowlifes. The style of fighting in America at this time was more of a "rough and tumble" style, devoid of skill or the science of boxing. The fights were brutal and were generally impromptu, staged when enough money was put up for the principles. To even survive to fight another day was considered a huge victory.

Over the next four years, it was here that Tom gained considerable notoriety and got the reputation of being the country's best. He fought many fights and it appears that he lost only once. Tom chased the one man to have defeated him all around New York, only to find that a rematch simply could not be made for one reason or another. It soon became clear that the fighter decided to officially "retire" from the prize ring in order to avoid a rematch with Molineaux. Although there is no surviving printed accounts of this or any of Molineaux's fights or purses while he was fighting in the United States, Molineaux must have been involved with enough of them to be the first man ever to have the title of "Champion of America" bestowed upon him.

Molineaux had forced the one man who beat him into retirement and had beaten all of the others that dared to enter the ring against him. But the English Sailors spoke of talented fighters back home, the popularity of Prize Fighting in England and the great amounts of money that could be made there. Intrigued, Tom took his title of "Champion of America" and set out for England to capture the World Title by beating the man who held the English Heavyweight Title, Tom Cribb.

Despite knowing few people and with the bulk of his ring earnings spent, Tom managed to get himself hired on as a ship's mate on board "The Bristol" for its return passage to Liverpool, England.   Just how Molineaux got aboard "The Bristol" is unknown as the ship and all of its manifest records sunk on December 16, 1819 near Wales' Porth Ysgo in Rhiw. Molineaux had no boating experience whatsoever. There have also been reports that he got aboard as a stow-away, but that is unlikely. Considering that he was a black man traveling by himself in the year 1809, if he had been found he most likely would have been thrown overboard into the sea. This was a long and dangerous trip from New York to London and it would have been virtually impossible for Molineaux to remain concealed should he have gotten on board without permission. The ships in those days were not very big and it would have been difficult for a full-grown man to hide for such a long journey while eating and drinking from very limited supplies.

There is also the possibility that Patrick Davis was still with Tom up to this point and it may have been Davis who helped land Molineaux a spot on "The Bristol" as a ship's mate.

After almost three difficult months as sea, and even times when he wished he was back on the Plantation in Virginia, Tom Molineaux arrived in London during the winter of 1809. He was penniless and alone. But not for long.

Soon after Tom landed on English soil he began to get recognition. At first, he was looked upon as a nut case. After all, the world was very different in 1809. Great Britain was the world's most powerful country and the United States   was in its infancy at just thirty-three years old. Slavery was still in full force in the States and despite England's much more open outlook on things they too were still very prejudiced against the black man. None of this seemed to bother Tom Molineaux. Here was a man, who we have to assume never had any formal education, no training of any kind, hadn't a friend or even an acquaintance at all in England, was flat broke and yet he was wandering the streets of London telling anyone who would listen that he was the champion of America. He was also considered physically imposing for that time, standing over five feet nine inches tall weighing between 196 and 200 lbs and sporting an Adonis-like physique. His dark skin and his "ugly" facial appearance added to the mystique that surrounded him. It's safe to say everyone who saw him, certainly noticed him! He visited the sporting houses and taverns boasting that he was the champion of America and could lick any man in England, including the Heavyweight Champion, Tom Cribb. He told everyone he came in contact with, whether they would listen or not, that he would fight anyone, but the main reason he came to England was to beat Cribb and become the Champion of England.

Everyone thought he was out of his mind, this crazed black man from America. After all, he was by himself without a penny in his pocket and he insisted on telling everyone in London that he intended to defeat Cribb and become the champion of England; Their England. A black man as the champion of England? Who was this American black to think he could come to the land where prizefighting began and become champion?

But the truth about boxing during that time was that it was in a serious lull. Cribb had not fought in a while and had been in semi-retirement because he had already beaten every worthy opponent. As much as the people thought of Molineaux as a whacko, they also seemed to enjoy the infusion of excitement he brought to the sporting circle, which was referred to as The

Fancy. The Fancy wanted and needed something to kick-start prizefighting again and many looked at Molineaux as that catalyst. Soon the sporting world began to notice Tom Molineaux. Most didn't think he could actually beat their Champion, but they found him amusing and as a result, Tom finally received some valuable information that got him pointed in the right direction.

He was told to seek out Bob Gregson, who was a popular Heavyweight and owned Bob's Chop House, which was a gathering place for the fight crowd. Tom found and met with Gregson at his Tavern. For whatever reason, be it the color of his skin, or his own evaluation, Bob didn't see any future for Molineaux and decided to send him to "one of his own." Gregson had another black fighter, who was also born in America, in mind and his name was Bill Richmond.

Chapter 3

Bill Richmond was born a slave in New York in 1763. While he was a teenager, he served Earl Percy, who was the commanding general of the British forces in New York during the American Revolution. Percy was impressed when he witnessed Richmond, who weighed around 160 lbs, take on and take out, not one, not two, but three men in a Tavern. Percy then had young Bill engage in several contests against New York based British Soldiers as entertainment for his guests.

When the war ended, Richmond stayed with Percy until he was sent to England to become a carpenter's apprentice in 1777. It was during his time in England that Bill honed his boxing skill. He developed his own style, which enabled him to side step or dodge the bull rush of his opponents and land effective counter-punches. By the late 1700s, Richmond was considered one of the best prizefighters around as he had victories over George Moore, Paddy Green and Frank Meyers; all top rate pugilists.

As the 19th century began, Richmond, even though he was over 40 years old, continued his prizefighting career winning enough fights to still be considered one of the top fighters of the age, which earned him a shot at another top fighter, Tom Cribb.

The fight between Bill Richmond and Tom Cribb took place on October 8, 1805 in Hailsham in Sussex. Despite giving away 18 years (Richmond was 42 and Cribb was 24) and over twenty pounds in weight, Richmond gave Cribb all he could handle. The fight however, was not exactly action-packed. As a matter of fact, because of Richmond's defensive skill, not a single, significant blow was landed in almost twenty minutes.

The crowd was virtually silent, except for the boos directed at Cribb who most in attendance expected to handle Bill Richmond with relative ease.

Cribb would bull rush Richmond only to have him side step the attack and return with sort of an "Ali-Shuffle" accompanied with taunting smiles. Bill's plan was to frustrate Tom Cribb and it was working. This routine continued for over ninety minutes. Many of the spectators had already gotten into their carriages and left shortly after the bout had started. As the snooze-fest continued and the remaining members of the Fancy began to exit, the umpire stopped the fight, raised Cribb's hand and declared him the winner.

Pearce Egan wrote: *"The Lily-White was milled in an hour and a half, with Cribb little worse for the Fray. He was unmarked on the outside but bleeding inside."*

Tom Cribb had been booed throughout the contest because many felt he should have disposed of Richmond rather easily. Cribb cursed Richmond for making him look like an erratic, talent-less novice. Cribb had won the fight, but lost the battle. This fight haunted Cribb and after collecting his share of the purse, he seriously considered retiring from the prize ring. But two years later, Tom Cribb beat Jem Belcher to become the Champion of England in a brutal fight that lasted thirty- five minutes.

Bill Richmond continued to fight as well, but was not as active as he once was in the ring. Instead, he became more involved in training and managing the younger fighters. (Note: Richmond continued to fight until 1818. After a third-round KO over Jack Carter, Richmond hung up the gloves at age 55 and focused on his Boxing Academy, which was located in London. He continued teaching the Sweet Science until his death on December 28, 1829. He was 66 years old.)

Despite not seeing any future in Tom, Bob Gregson felt the only way to aid Molineaux or simply unload him, was to seek out Bill Richmond based on his race and reputation. Richmond lived at the Horse & Dolphin on St. Martins Street in Leicester Square. Soon Tom arrived at Richmond's place and said that he would be taking up residence and proceeded to "make himself at home." Molineaux told Bill that his only purpose for coming to England was to beat Tom Cribb for the Championship of England and that he wanted Bill to set up the fight. He was also very vocal about his belief in his own ability of beating any man that would set foot inside the ring with him. Molineaux had no money and no friends in England, yet he seemed to draw a crowd wherever he went. The Horse & Dolphin was no different. People were listening to him talk and didn't know what to expect. He looked imposing, but no one had ever seen him fight in or out of the ring. All they had to go by was what Tom was saying. He wanted food and drink and a roof over his head but did not have a penny. All he had were his words and dreams of winning the championship of England.

Richmond fed Tom and agreed to let him stay at the Horse & Dolphin. But despite Molineaux's confidence in himself, Bill Richmond wasn't convinced that Tom would be a worthy opponent for the Champion. After seeing Molineaux in person, Richmond could tell he was in shape, but early on he thought the same as Gregson did; No future. Richmond did feel some sort of kinship towards the American, but thought that Molineaux could very well be out of his mind.

However, being a smart businessman, Richmond thought that Molineaux was a novelty and figured he might be able to make a little money off of him so he decided to take him in as his new fighter. After watching Tom train, he became even less impressed. His style was crude and he was far from displaying the science of boxing. However, his physical makeup was impressive and Richmond thought if he could break Tom of his American style of fighting and teach him the sweet science, maybe he could win a few fights on English soil. Richmond tried to teach Tom how to jab and to throw his right hand behind it. He also tried to break Molineaux of the way he was delivering his punches, which was in a downward motion, striking with the bottom of his clenched fist rather than landing a punch with his knuckles. This type of "Hammer" punch was common in America, but would not fare well against the more scientific fighters in England.

By this time, everyone had heard of Tom Molineaux and rumors of a 5' 9" tall Negro from America, who had bulging muscles, was as strong as a bull and had outstretched arms that were two yards long. The talk among The Fancy was that he showed signs of beating any man, including Tom Cribb. Robert Barclay was a rich gambler who was Tom Cribb's manager, trainer and promoter. When the rumors of this 26- year old black behemoth reached Barclay's ears, he had to see Tom for himself. After all, he liked the sound of a black vs. white match-up and could see that considerable profit could be made for such a bout. Tom Cribb was the champion of England. How could a black man from America, a former slave no less, possess the skill and power to wrestle the title from him? It seemed like nonsense and he thought that the sporting world had to be over estimating his abilities.

Barclay got word that Richmond had been training Molineaux and offered to spar the man himself. Barclay was in good shape and never trained, or boxed in any way other than one hundred percent; sparring to him was a real fight. He sparred many times with Cribb and he had fights with Pearce and Jem Belcher as well. Barclay set up the sparring session to take place at Jackson's Gym. When he arrived at the gym, he was surprised to see that not only was Tom Molineaux already there, primed and ready to go, he was wearing Barclay's favorite "mufflers" (Note: Mufflers were a type of boxing glove that the bare-knuckle fighters of the time sparred with to protect their hands). It pissed Barclay off seeing Molineaux wearing the mufflers everyone knew belonged on his fists but Barclay didn't say a word. Instead, he borrowed someone else's, stripped, loosened up, and he was ready to go. Barclay had decided that he would take out his anger on the American black. After the two shook hands, the sparring session began.

Barclay was not really expecting much in terms of Tom's boxing ability but was immediately surprised when Tom started the match smiling at him. Without a setup move or warning of any kind, Molineaux launched what he later referred to as "a cotton-picking-haymaker-punch" that landed right in the old bread basket of Barclay with such force that he splintered not one but two of Barclay's upper ribs! Barclay collapsed in agony and the session was over. Two sounds were heard in the gym that day. The first was the heavy thud of the impact of Tom's punch as it landed to Barclay's mid-section and the other was the sound of Barclay crashing to the floor. Barclay was not only hurt, but extremely embarrassed. He pulled himself up, regained his composure and left the gym. When he was able, he sent word to Tom Cribb that he had better take a look at the American black.

Bill Richmond and Molineaux continued to train. Bill could see improvement and was pleased with the interest in learning the Sweet Science that Tom displayed. It was all business as the two worked extremely hard day after day. The days turned into weeks and weeks into months and after working with Tom all winter and into the spring, Richmond felt that Molineaux was ready for his first fight in England. Molineaux still had a lot to learn and still possessed much of his "bad American habits" but he had reached a point where he needed to fight a real opponent.

Bill began looking around for a suitable opponent for Tom. He knew that Tom believed in his own ability and thought he could beat anyone, but Richmond also knew that   despite working so hard for the past several months, and learning a great deal, it was still unclear how much Molineaux had learned and how much he had improved. Richmond needed to find an opponent that would definitely test Molineaux. But he also knew that it was critical in Tom's development to secure a victory before he could advance to better opposition and ultimately continue his preparation for a possible shot at Tom Cribb and his title. After carefully looking for an opponent for over two months there were still no takers. Richmond had to put out the word in a big way that his young protégé would fight ANY inferior man, which meant that he was willing to fight anyone except someone of championship caliber.

Meanwhile, the popularity around Molineaux continued to grow. Wherever he went, people would surround him. They could not get enough of Tom Molineaux. Everyone in the sporting world wanted to be around him. This included women, white women. Molineaux basked in his newfound fame. He loved every minute of the attention he was getting. As Tom enjoyed himself after the hard workouts, Richmond continued his search for Tom's first fight.

Soon it would be Tom Cribb, of all people, who approached Bill Richmond with an offer to fight one of HIS fighters. Cribb told Richmond that the fighter he had in mind was a novice and had never been involved in a real prize ring contest. He said that he had been involved with several sparring sessions but that was it. Richmond thought this was the perfect test for Molineaux and agreed to the fight at a purse of 50 pounds per side.

Molineaux's FIRST fight in England took place at Tothill Fields in Westminster on July 24, 1810 against a 6' foot tall, 210 pound Bristolean named Jack Burrows. Tom Cribb trained Jack who, aside from his famous instructor, was virtually unknown. As a matter of fact, many referred to him as "The Bristol Unknown." By this time there was a considerable amount of interest in Molineaux, but of the three hundred spectators gathered to see –The New Black‖ as he was being called, none really knew what to expect. When Molineaux stripped his 5′ 9″, 196 lb frame to get ready for the contest, a collective sigh was heard as all in attendance saw Tom's skin glistening with sweat and his muscles bulging with his every movement. There was no doubt that Tom was in top shape. To this point, no one like Tom had been seen before on English soil. As popular as he had become, and as inquisitive as people had been about him, not many of the 300 or so spectators in attendance really thought that Tom could win. After all, how could a barbaric black from America best a boxing student of the champion of England who seemed the bigger and stronger man?

Tom Cribb and his brother George worked Burrows' corner, while Bill Richmond and a man known only as Clarke, worked Molineaux's. As the fight began, slightly before 7:00 am, all of the questions concerning Tom Molineaux were answered and answered quickly.

Tom dominated the fight from the outset. Burrows was game (showed heart) and continued to come at Molineaux, who in return routinely landed blow after blow with extreme force. The impact of every punch that Tom landed caused damage. Burrows landed some very hard shots to the head of Molineaux but none seemed to inflict any damage and all in attendance learned that Tom could not only deliver a devastating shot to his opponent, he could also take a punch. The fight lasted for sixty-five minutes and was action-packed. Molineaux punished Burrows so bad, that it was impossible to distinguish a single feature on his face. Despite his crude style, Tom showed his strength and he received considerable attention from all of the spectators who immediately viewed him as a pugilist of promise. With Molineaux surging and Burrows unable to breathe and struggling to see through eyes that were swollen shut, Tom Cribb was forced, very much to his dismay, to throw in the sponge.

Immediately after the fight, Cribb approached Bill Richmond and complained that Tom had fouled Burrows. Bill took offense to this accusation and after an exchange of a few words the two men started to fight. Both men landed a few hard punches, but then stopped, realizing they were fighting for free and THAT was not going to happen. In that six or seven minutes of action, not only did Tom Molineaux get to see the man he traveled over 3000 miles to fight, he got to see him in action as well.

Among the rather small crowd, there was an important gentleman present, Lord George Sackville, a younger brother of the Duke of Dorset. He was very impressed with Molineaux and his performance. He said that the black was equal to any fighter he had seen and felt he could not only challenge Cribb for his title, he felt he could win. He was so confident of this that he approached Bill Richmond and promised that if he could get Tom another battle with a first- class fighter and win; he would put up the money for the black to fight for the championship.

Bill Richmond was pleased with Tom's performance to a degree. The only reason why Molineaux did not finish off his opponent sooner was due to his lack of "science." Despite working on the correct way to deliver a punch, Tom continued to use his "Hammer Blow," which gave Richmond something to make sure his new pupil would correct before his next fight. One other thing was accomplished during Tom's first fight on English soil; he got his first view of the reason why he came to England in the first place, English champion, Tom Cribb. Likewise, Cribb was able to get his first look at Molineaux. After hearing all of the rumors and seeing Tom in action first hand, Cribb was not at all impressed.

After his conversation with Richmond, Lord George Sackville did not hide his feelings about Molineaux, telling all of The Fancy that Tom was the equal of any man on the British Isles and that he has officially offered to back Molineaux in his quest to unseat Tom Cribb as the English champion. Finally, there was some excitement back in prizefighting and Molineaux was the reason for it.

When Richmond got Tom back to the Horse & Dolphin, they retired into a back room. Bill talked to his young fighter for several hours telling him that despite winning the contest, he still showed that he had a lot to learn and a long way to go if he wanted to challenge Tom Cribb for the Title. He also enlightened Tom that although many of The Fancy sung his praises, the more experienced ones saw his weaknesses. Richmond told Molineaux that if he had incorporated more of what the two had been practicing, he would have dispatched Burrows much sooner and the only reason the fight pressed on, was due to the fact he was not setting up his powerful right hands behind a jab. Instead, he reverted back to his –Hammer Blow,‖ which was something he simply had to stop doing. Richmond added that Tom was still not utilizing Richmond's side-step moves to avoid his opponent's rushes and punches and although Tom displayed the ability to absorb a lot of punishment, this would fail him as he stepped up and fought more experienced fighters. Tom said he understood. Richmond told Molineaux that he needed to spend more time breaking his bad habits and that he had to focus on the techniques that the two had been practicing and working so hard at for the past several months.

Tom was anxious to improve and wanted to get back into the gym and begin training at once, but Richmond told him he needed to rest for the remainder of the day and night. Richmond explained that despite not showing any signs of injury, prize fighting will dish out damage to his body and that he needed to give it time to rest and in most cases, even despite seeing no physical damage, he needed time to heal. Bill told Tom that the rest of the night was his to enjoy in the Tavern.

When the two emerged from the privacy of the back room and entered the Tavern, Tom got his first taste of what it was like to be truly regarded as a top-rate pugilist by members of The Fancy. He also felt what it was like to be the toast-of-the-town and to have the sports push each other out of the way so they could treat Tom to as much food and drink as he could handle. Tom also found that the women were very anxious to be with him and they were not hiding their feelings in public, which was very uncommon during that time. Most women suddenly desired Tom Molineaux; he was the talk-of-the-town and had become extremely popular in the eyes of the sporting and non-sporting worlds.

It was official; Tom Molineaux was a celebrity.

Chapter 4

Bill Richmond knew that despite his recent success, Molineaux was still very crude when it came to the science of boxing. He emphasized to Tom how important it was for him to learn the finer points of prize fighting if he truly wanted to prepare himself to challenge Tom Cribb for the Heavyweight Title. Molineaux continued to train and work on his boxing technique with Richmond and Bill fine-tuned Tom's skills. Under Richmond's tutelage, Molineaux began to learn how to fight at the correct distance from his opponent. Richmond taught him that by delivering a blow from the proper distance it would inflict more damage. Molineaux learned quickly and in a short period of time was able to deliver his blows using the proper distance. He discovered that when he delivered either a jab or a power punch, it was more effective when thrown from the proper position. Molineaux loved to learn new ways to make himself a better fighter. And while Tom worked on using distance to help his offensive attack, Richmond felt it was time to introduce another dimension of distance to help him become a better boxer.

Bill Richmond had fought and lost to Tom Cribb. That was the bad news. The good news was that during his fight with Cribb, he was virtually untouched by the Champion. His defensive skills aided him that day when his own offensive attack lacked the firepower required to beat Tom Cribb. Richmond knew Molineaux had the firepower to de-throne the champion, but he also knew that Tom lacked the defensive skill required to avoid the offensive charges he would receive when he stepped into the ring with Cribb. Bill needed to teach Tom how to combine the effectiveness of distance while attacking his opponent as well as a form of defense for when he is under attack.

Richmond and his star pupil began to focus on using distance to help Tom's defense. Molineaux learned to increase the fluidness of his footwork to help with avoiding punches. He was taught to move smoothly during sparring, rather than plod towards or away from his opponent. After putting in endless hours of work practicing relentlessly in the gym with Richmond on defensive distance as well as counter-punching when spaced correctly from his opponent for an offensive advantage, it finally clicked for Molineaux! He now understood and could apply the correct distance during sparring that helped him improve both offensively and defensively. For the first time during his prizefighting career, Molineaux had finally learned how to use his natural strength and agility as an asset inside the ring.

To this point, Richmond was pleased with his student. He felt that Tom had progressed enough with distance and he was ready to learn how to utilize his quick and powerful left. Richmond taught Tom how to snap his left out as a jab and because of Tom's power, when the blows landed they would inflict damage on the target. Again, Molineaux learned quickly and Bill was happy with his young fighter's progress. As he'd done with distance, Richmond showed Tom how to use his left jab both defensively and as an offensive weapon. Bill showed Tom how to use his left as protection by defensively blocking punches thrown at him. Because Tom had such fast reflexes, he was able to apply the defensive side of his jab in half the time it took him to learn how to deliver it as an effective blow. Molineaux was becoming the complete package under the guidance of Bill Richmond. He had it all; youth, power, speed, agility and stamina. He was learning how to put it all together and use it to his advantage inside the squared circle. It was becoming obvious to most observers that Tom Molineaux was indeed blossoming into a legitimate challenger to Tom Cribb's Crown.

As good as Molineaux was getting, and despite his confidence in himself as well as the confidence most members of The Fancy had in Molineaux's current skill level, Bill Richmond knew there was one more piece of the puzzle that Tom had to not only learn, he had to master.

One advantage Richmond had going for him while he was teaching Molineaux the science of boxing was that Tom Molineaux was blessed with a lot of natural stamina, strength and agility. Molineaux was being taught to utilize his strengths and the result was that he was becoming a very good athlete. Many fighters of the era learned to fight but few were athletes. The main goal of prizefighters during that period was to have plenty of stamina as well as the ability to take a punch. Most fighters of the day had a punch, otherwise they didn't enter into the prize ring to begin with, so they concentrated on being able to sustain an attack for long periods of time and at the same time having the ability to weather the storm from their opponents. Molineaux was a young fighter that possessed all of the most important traits needed to be a very good prizefighter. Bill Richmond taught Tom how to use his natural abilities in a controlled way to help him become more refined in the finer points of the sweet science. Tom Molineaux had become a fighter who could do more than just fight. Molineaux went into training with Richmond as a rough and tumble scrapper but emerged as an athlete who seemed to be able to do it all. Tom was able to move quickly in all directions and once he was taught how to run and breathe correctly, he ran long distances and short sprints with ease. He could deliver punches as well as defend them with his left hand.

And now that Tom could recognize distance to deliver and avoid punches and he was able to use his left jab effectively, the final skill Tom had to learn and master was using his right hand; his big right was the last un-refined asset Tom Molineaux possessed.

To define Tom's right as being powerful would be a gross understatement. The simple fact that he broke a man's ribs with a single blow when he did NOT know how to deliver a punch says it all. Now Tom knew how to deliver his punches. Richmond knew that if Molineaux had any chance of dethroning Tom Cribb as England's Heavyweight champion, he had to be able to not only deliver his powerful right, it had to land hard, land clean and land often.

As the important first step, Richmond showed Tom how to use his left jab in order to setup his devastating right. Richmond also taught Molineaux how to use his left jab to break down his opponent's own defense in order to follow it with meaningful and accurate right hand punches with KO power.

Molineaux enjoyed the fruits of his schooling. He enjoyed delivering power shots that would render a man unconscious with a single blow. Molineaux became a complete fighter under Bill Richmond. He could now deliver blows from multiple angles with power in either hand and at the same time, use his quickness to avoid return punches. He learned how to take advantage of an opponent who threw and missed him with a punch by counter-punching using either his right or left hand. Molineaux was developing nicely and Bill Richmond felt he was ready for another fight but this time, a stern test was needed. Fighting in the gym was one thing, but fighting a quality opponent when money was at stake was definitely another. So Richmond began to seek out a quality opponent for Tom's next contest.

As Bill looked for a quality bout for Molineaux, Tom was receiving a lot of attention and was enjoying his new celebrity status at Richmond's Horse & Dolphin Tavern. He received his first taste of fame from the diverse crowd that frequented the pub, which included the rich, the poor, the young and the old. What drew them all together was the love of sport. With his recent impressive victory over Burrows, and the fact that

Tom was an imposing black man, who stood out no matter where he went, he became the "spice" of prizefighting. With his recent performance and his obvious improvements he made in the gym, he added life to the sport, which was going through a serious lull.

Tom Cribb, the English heavyweight champion, was in a semi-retirement because he felt no other active fighter to be worthy of a shot at his crown. Many had begun to think that Tom Molineaux was a worthy opponent for the champion and there also were a large number of them that felt Molineaux could actually defeat Cribb. The potential match-up between Tom Molineaux and Tom Cribb was a popular conversation. Whether each member of the sporting world felt Molineaux would defeat Cribb or not, Tom Molineaux was viewed by most as being good for the game. Molineaux, who had never known anything of celebrity, was enjoying every minute of the attention he was receiving. He could eat, drink, and have the best cigars handed to him from fans that just wanted to be in his presence in return. Tom began to enjoy his celebrity too much, especially when it came to the drink.

Not only was the sports world fascinated with Tom, he had also piqued the interest of London's women. Most, whether White, black, married, single, young, old, princess or prostitute, most made no bones about the fact they had desires for "The New Black Celebrity Prizefighter" and Tom loved every minute of it. Tom was having the time of his life, doing things that he had only dreamed of in the past. Molineaux was often seen with women on each arm and two or more following close by as he strolled down the streets. These weren't just any old streets; these were the streets of London, one of the most modern cities in the world!

Boxing was booming and as good as Molineaux was for prizefighting, the women and booze was not good for Tom Molineaux. Bill Richmond knew that Tom's new found celebrity could mean trouble but he did nothing about it. Tom worked hard in training and rather than hold his young fighter back from the vices that were known to have a negative influence on young fighters, Richmond chose to let Molineaux loose in the evening while he continued to seek out his next opponent. After all, Bill Richmond was learning something throughout all of this too. Bill learned that Tom Molineaux had become a cash cow for him and his pub. The Horse & Dolphin had never been so crowded as it had become since Tom's victory over Burrows, followed by the boasting and backing by Lord George Sackville. In order to keep the ale flowing and the pub packed, Molineaux had to be made available. If that meant Tom spending too much time with the ladies, drinking too much booze and smoking too many stogies with the gents, then so be it. After all, Molineaux was young and was still performing exceptionally in the gym and most importantly to Richmond, business was business and Tom Molineaux was becoming very profitable.

Bill Richmond continued searching relentlessly for a quality opponent that would test his young fighter. He felt that Molineaux needed to be challenged enough for him to apply all he had learned during these tough weeks of training. Richmond knew that the goal was to get Tom Cribb into the ring, but he also felt that Molineaux was not 100% ready. Richmond needed someone who was very good offensively and he also had to be durable.

Richmond finally found the right opponent. His name was Tom Blake and he carried the nickname "Tough Tom." Bill Richmond had found Molineaux's next foe; "Tough Tom" was perfect.

Blake was a sailor and as his nickname suggested a real tough guy. He was an experienced fighter who possessed stamina, heart and strength and would be a perfect gauge to see how good Molineaux really was.

Tough Tom was considered to be one of the very best fighters of his era according to Pierce Egan. Egan wrote that when discussing quality fighters of the age, Blake had to be mentioned as he was known to have fought most of the quality fighters of the time.

Pierce Egan describes Blake in Boxiana II, which was first published in 1812: *–His combats have not only been numerous but uniformly good ~ remarkably dexterous and scientific upon all occasions, and possessing a bottom* (which meant stamina and courage) *of the finest quality that rendered him a tremendous competitor to all those who had the temerity to enter the lists with him: and it must not be passed over, that the greatest CHEFS* (top fighters) *of the present period found it of the utmost difficulty to make him pronounce the word Enough!"*

On January 30, 1804 Blake entered the ring with Jack Holmes, who was considered one of the top fighters of the day. The fight was a brutal contest that lasted sixty rounds. During the twenty-ninth round, Blake sprained his knee so bad, he could barely stand, however he fought on. During the sixtieth and final round, Tough Tom unleashed an attack that had Holmes so beaten he was about to go, but then unleashed a fury of his own that put Blake in trouble. But, due to fatigue, Holmes was not able to finish off Tough Tom and once more the tables turned in favor of Blake, as he pounded Jack Holmes until he was reluctantly forced to give in, giving the victory to Tom Blake.

During the spring of 1805, Tom Blake got a shot at Tom Cribb's title and pushed the Champion to his limits as the fight lasted for over an hour and a half before the tough Sailor reluctantly admitted defeat.

When Richmond found him, "Tough Tom" had just returned from spending several years at sea and was as hard as nails, with a composition that was preserved by life on the sea. While at sea, Tough Tom Blake fought several fights; he was in shape and eager to give "The New Black" a try. All that was preventing Blake from securing the fight was the 100 guineas required from each side. Once again, the champion of England, Tom Cribb got involved and put up the money so the fight would take place. And in less than one month after his first fight on English soil, a few miles from Margate at Epple Bay, Molineaux was set for his next fight at the Castle Tavern, on August 21, 1810.

After word of Molineaux's first bout and his newfound fame, and then his constant belittling and calling out of Tom Cribb, there was a considerable amount of interest in the Molineaux versus Blake fight. On the day of the contest, all types of vehicles, (horse drawn buggies & carriages) as well as many fans on foot blocked the road on the way to the location of the fight. Most could not wait to see just how much Tom Molineaux had improved. As it approached noon, it was already a blistering hot day. Many of the spectators began to protect themselves from the sun while Tom Molineaux seemed to be thoroughly enjoying the conditions as he made his way to the ring, anxious to get the fight started. "Tough Tom" made his entrance seated in a baronet's barouche and finally joined Molineaux inside the ring.

Molineaux was seconded by Bill Richmond and "Tough Tom" had Tom Cribb as his second and Bill Gibbons as his bottle-holder. Both fighters met at the center of the ring, shook hands and got ready to begin this much-anticipated contest.

In the first round, Molineaux's improved boxing skill was apparent right away, as the two combatants sparred with each other during the first part of the round until Molineaux landed several devastating "Hammer Blows" to the back of Tough Tom's head, sending him down to end the first round.

At the start of the second round, Blake came at Molineaux in an attempt of ending the bout, but learned that although he was still somewhat crude, he was no easy opponent. Molineaux was able to apply his newfound skill as he successfully knocked down Blake's guard with his left hand, and landed several powerful rights until one so tremendous; it sent Blake down to end the round.

When round three began, Molineaux could see that Blake was tired and moved in viscously with an offensive attack. But being the veteran he was, Tough Tom was ready. Blake was able to avoid several direct shots and was able to counter- punch and land a few hard punches of his own. As Molineaux moved in to throw a right, Blake landed a powerful shot to his chin but despite receiving a solid punch on the jaw, Molineaux was simply not fazed. By the end of the third round, Tough Tom was exhausted and ultimately went down from a power shot that would have ended the fight for most right then, but Tom Blake was not known as Tough Tom for nothing.

The fight continued and the fourth round saw Molineaux land many devastating blows to the face of Tough Tom, who landed several solid shots to the body of Molineaux in return, but none seemed to affect "The New Black" at all. The two combatants grabbed each other and both fell to the ground, with Molineaux landing on top of Blake to end the round.

By the time a minute had passed to begin the fifth, Blake's entire face was covered in blood and he was visibly tired, but due to his great resolution, Tough Tom rallied and unleashed a barrage of punches on Molineaux. But once again, it was to no avail. Molineaux was able to regain the momentum by holding Blake's neck in his left arm, while pounding at his face with his right until Tough Tom dropped to the dirt to end the round.

The sixth was all Molineaux as he consistently and with ease, knocked down the guard of Blake with his left and followed up with solid rights until Tom Blake went down to end the stanza. As Blake was dragged back to his corner, he was gasping for air and was completely covered in blood. It seemed to everyone in attendance that he was unable to hurt Molineaux at all.

During the seventh round, despite fatigue, Tough Tom Blake toughened, refusing to give in, regardless of the beating he was sustaining, and once again was able to rally with an offensive assault. But again, Blake was just too weak to do the damage he needed to do in order to drop the seemingly invincible Molineaux. The seventh ended when due to the combination of fatigue and a few solid shots landed by Molineaux, Blake went down.

As soon as the eighth round started, it was obvious Molineaux was looking to end the fight. He came out with a fury, throwing and landing many punches as Blake tried to retreat and cover up. Molineaux ended things abruptly with a devastating punch to the head of Blake, which sent him down and kept him down, unable to recover in the time allotted, giving Molineaux his second victory in a row on English soil.

If Tom Molineaux was officially introduced to The Fancy during his first fight in England against Burrows, then his performance against Tough Tom Blake solidified Molineaux's claim that he had indeed been worthy of a shot at Tom Crib and the heavyweight championship in his second.

Pierce Egan was ringside for the Molineaux-Blake contest and wrote, *"In the above battle the amateurs were completely astonished at the improvement exhibited by Molineaux, and the punishment he dealt out was so truly tremendous and his strength and bottom so superior, that he was deemed a proper match for the Champion."*

Henry Miles who covered the fight for "Pugilistica" shared his thoughts.   Miles wrote, *"In this battle Molineaux evinced great improvement in the science of pugilism, particularly in the art of giving, while nature seemed to have endowed him abundantly with the gift of taking, his body being almost callous to fistic punishment.   It was generally considered that should he be able to combine an equal degree of skill with his gluttony, he would mill the whole race of modern pugilists."*

At the conclusion of the fight, Tom was almost unmarked, despite taking several hard punches from Tom Blake. The only sign that Molineaux had even been in a prizefight at all was a small cut under one of his eyes.

Afterwards, most boxing fans felt that Molineaux not only improved greatly from his last fight a month before, but they now felt that Molineaux would give England's heavyweight champion a tough contest. Also increasing in number were members of The Fancy who honestly felt that Molineaux could not only give Tom Cribb a good fight, he could beat him.

Perhaps caught up in the moment, or in the praise everyone was giving Tom Molineaux, Bill Richmond thought that his student did have a chance, a very good chance.

Richmond felt it was time for Molineaux to officially challenge Tom Cribb for the Heavyweight Championship of England.

Chapter 5

Molineaux was quite the buzz around the sporting world. The masses were talking of him as not only a worthy opponent for the champion; many felt he could actually beat Cribb. To this point, the interest in Tom Molineaux was more for amusement; the oddity of it; but after his victory over Blake, the reality of Molineaux potentially winning the title became painfully evident to most Englishmen. All of a sudden, the Honor of England was at stake!

Tom Cribb had been in a semi "retirement" because he felt there were no worthy opponents for him. He felt he had beaten them all and had nothing left to prove. Now, the public felt there was a worthy opponent and his name was Tom Molineaux. At first, Cribb stated that he had no intentions of "coming back" despite Molineaux's official challenge. When Cribb's comment spread throughout the boxing world, Richmond had Molineaux quickly make an official response and demand that if Cribb would not fight him, then he, Tom Molineaux, should be considered the champion of England.

This was no joke. For Cribb what started out as seeing if there actually was a fighter on the horizon that could possibly wrestle the title from him, now became a major concern. After all, Molineaux was an American, and to make matters worse, he was a black American. Now the honor of the country was definitely at stake. Cribb was refusing to fight the black and the rumblings to have Tom Molineaux crowned champion began to get louder and louder thanks to Bill Richmond.

As the pieces seemed to fall in place for Molineaux, Bill Richmond continued to make the right business decisions. He started a public campaign to have Tom recognized as the champion. Both Molineaux and Richmond were very busy. Molineaux was spending time with The Fancy, while Richmond was working the public through the press with a carefully planned and calculated promotional campaign that would equal that of the great Don King.

The more successful Richmond was schmoozing with the press and public, the more Molineaux was exposed to drinking and hanging out with as many women as he could. He spent every penny he had on fine clothes and enjoyed the attention he received as he was frequently seen with several pretty women at a time. He was not training as much as he had been and just couldn't say no to the offer of a great smoke, the best spirits or the attentions of a fine woman.

During this era of boxing, most fighters did not participate in regular training regiments. If they could take a beating, and had a punch, it was enough. Several fighters of the day went on a special diet for a week or two leading up to a scheduled match, but for the most part, most prizefighters did not do anything special to prepare themselves for matches. But, Richmond was an advocate of training and rigorous preparation, and as a result, Molineaux had benefited. Tom Cribb also knew the value of training. He knew how important it was to get his body in the best shape possible to endure the punishment one takes fighting at the championship level.

Cribb had seen Molineaux fight up close. Although he was not overly impressed, there was no denying that the black was in phenomenal shape and Cribb knew that he needed the extra time in order to get himself into top shape. He hadn't been in a prizefight in years. And he hadn't trained in years either.

The promotional campaign continued on, as did much talk of the fight, and the match just had to take place! Finally, after public pressure from the sporting world and from countrymen who felt he had to stand up for England itself, Tom Cribb agreed to fight Molineaux to ensure the championship remained in its rightful place, England. But Cribb had a single condition. He demanded that the fight take place in December, which was much further off than Bill Richmond wanted to wait.

The talk of when and where the mega-fight of the time would be set continued on for several weeks. The truth was that after all the challenges and boasts that had been coming from Tom Molineaux's own lips about how he could lick any man on the planet including the champion, etc., etc. etc., Richmond had little choice of when the fight should take place. Richmond knew that the fight was to be set when Cribb wanted, so he waited for an official announcement of the contest. In the meantime, Cribb began training. Molineaux began his training as well, but was not as dedicated to it as he had been. His dedication was to partying with his fan base and spending time with his lady base now seemed to be the top priority in his life.

But by the fall the fight was made official. Both sides put up the required money, which was 200 Guineas each and agreed that the fight would happen, as Cribb demanded, in December 1810.

Bill Richmond desperately tried to convince Molineaux that he needed to use the extra time leading up to the fight to continue to train hard in the gym. Richmond tried to emphasize to his young fighter that Cribb did not become the champion by accident and that Cribb's own style, skill and stamina would take Molineaux to the absolute limit. But Molineaux truly believed that no one on the planet, including the Champion himself, could beat him in a prizefight. Tom's two prior experiences with fighters on English soil did not push him to any limit whatsoever and whether Tom's arrogance or his simple-minded thinking made him assume that all fighters in England, including Tom Cribb himself, would not give him much trouble. It still remained to be seen, but the fact was, Tom Molineaux did indeed think he was invincible. He also began to think that the hardest training was behind him. After all, it was a lot more fun to eat and drink with the sports all day and hang with the ladies all night. When did he have time to train?

Tom Cribb was a quality fighter. He had been in many battles and had proved to be one of the best the sport had seen. He was known for his skill at "fighting on the retreat," which we would look at today as a fighter who can box-on-the-move. He was able to land a blow and then move quickly out of the way of his opponent's punches. But despite his unique ability to fight while moving, Cribb was also well known for his ability to absorb huge amounts of punishment, which clearly set him apart from the other great fighters of his era. Cribb simply would not quit. He had only done so one time before and that was when he was young. Tom Cribb had been considered unbeatable by most; that is until Tom Molineaux arrived in England.

So Cribb trained hard, but many close to him felt that he was not really taking Tom Molineaux too seriously. Cribb did feel that Molineaux was much too inexperienced to better him in a prizefight. Cribb resolved that if he got into decent shape, it would be enough to beat the black without much trouble.

And many of Cribb's backers felt the same way. They were very confident that their man Tom would beat Molineaux the black, and offered large odds that the fight would not last fifteen minutes.

As the fight date drew closer, the talk was all over England. The tension for both sides grew each day. It seemed that everyone, not just the sporting types, or The Fancy, everyone in England was interested in this fight.

One report by an unknown writer in a London paper wrote, *"In London clubs and sporting taverns, on the stock exchange and in the village alehouses, amongst West-end swells and East-end roughs, nothing was talked of but the fight between Cribb and Molineaux".*

Henry Miles wrote, *"The affair excited the most extraordinary sensation, not only in the pugilistic world, but also among the classes who had hitherto considered boxing as beneath their notice and who now thinking the honor of their country was at stake, took a most lively interest in the affair."*

During a pouring rain, both Team Molineaux and Team Cribb arrived the night before the scheduled event in the Grinstead neighborhood. Cribb's backers and the rest of his corner stayed at the Crown House. Molineaux, Richmond and the rest of their team stayed at the Dorset Arms. Despite the awful weather, the town was packed and filled with much excitement and anticipation of the next day's scheduled match-up. Both Teams settled in for the night.

The fight took place at Copthall Common in East Grinstead, Sussex, which was about thirty miles outside of London, on December 18, 1810. The weather on the day of the fight was worse than the previous night. It was simply terrible. The temperature was cold, just around the freezing mark and it was raining steadily. The rain, which was a freezing rain, was described as "coming down in torrents." Despite the unfavorable conditions, and the distance from the Metropolis, over 10,000 fans showed up to witness what was being referred to as "The World Prizefighting Championship."

The crowd in attendance, which featured every possible class represented in society from Royalty to people living on the streets, trudged through knee-deep mud for over five miles to get a spot on the hillside where the fight would take place.

The Master of Ceremonies was Gentleman John Jackson. Jackson was usually the man in charge of the biggest events of the time. As was his duty as the Master of Ceremonies, Gentleman John Jackson began to pitch the ring. Jackson first created an outer ring at the bottom of a hill, which he etched into the ground and then had roped off for crowd control. Then the inside ring where the fight would take place, was formed with a twenty-four foot area roped off.

As soon as the ring was set and ready to go, which was a little after noon, the principles were told to get ready to set-to. Molineaux immediately stepped out of the carriage where he had been waiting and bowed to the crowd. Despite the pouring, freezing rain, and the gusts of wind and over 10,000 spectators in attendance, the roar of silence was utterly deafening. He made his way to the ring and tossed his cap into the center of the ring, waited a few seconds, and then jumped over the rope into the ring.

Moments later, Tom Cribb appeared standing on top of a carriage. The crowd went wild. The roar of over 10,000 strong made the hillside rumble. Cribb made his way through the hundreds of outstretched hands and pats on the back. After what seemed to take forever, both fighters and their seconds were in the ring. The cheers finally died down and all that could be heard were the odds being yelled back and forth. Considerable odds were being given that Cribb would dispose of Molineaux inside of fifteen minutes and even odds were given for a Tom Cribb victory inside thirty minutes.

The referee in charge of the action was Sir Thomas Apreece and the two appointed umpires were Lord Archibald Hamilton and Colonel Barton. Molineaux was seconded by Bill Richmond and Paddington Jones. Tom Cribb's seconds were John Gully and Joe Ward.

Cribb yelled to his backers that the fight would not exceed fifteen minutes and the first round of ale at the Crown House was on him! Molineaux said nothing. As both fighters stripped and prepared to fight, everyone in attendance got to see the contrast in both combatants. Cribb was taller and was heavier, making him the larger man, however Molineaux's superior physique and muscle tone made him appear the more powerful of the two men.

Henry Miles wrote, *"Upon stripping the appearance of the men was really formidable; Cribb, who stood at five feet ten inches and a half, weighed fourteen stone three pounds, while Molineaux, who was five feet eight inches and a quarter was only a pound lighter, and consequently looked more muscular. His arms were of wondrous length and roundness of form. He looked confident and fierce, rather than smiling, and nodded his head as the two men again shook hands."*

As Molineaux and Cribb met and shook hands in the center of the ring, you could feel the energy throughout the crowd. The fight that everyone had been waiting for was about to begin. Both fighters signaled that they were ready and Sir Thomas Apreece ordered the fighters to set-to by yelling TIME!

The first round was a feeling-out round. Both fighters landed a few shots, sparring back and forth. Molineaux landed a solid left followed by a hard right to the head of Cribb. The Champion had some problems finding the right distance, but landed a timed left under the eye of Molineaux. After an exchange of shots, Molineaux was thrown down to end the round.

The second round began with Molineaux landing a hard left to Cribb's head. Cribb answered with a powerful left of his own which landed on Tom's right eyebrow. To the astonishment of all in attendance, this punch virtually had no effect on Molineaux. Tom returned with a flurry of shots including a powerful right that caused Cribb's teeth to chatter as it opened up a cut on Cribb's mouth. Molineaux drew first blood, which was one of the major highlights of prizefights during this era. There was always a substantial amount of money wagered on who drew the first blood and who-ever had wagered on the black to draw first blood that day won a considerable amount of money, as Cribb was the heavy favorite to be the one to do it. At the close of the round, the odds were four to one in favor of Cribb.

As the third round began, both fighters stood toe-to-toe and sparred. Cribb displayed the superior science, but Tom had improved significantly since his last fight with Blake. The round ended when a solid body shot thrown by Cribb landed under Molineaux's rib, sending him down to a knee.

The fourth did not last long as Cribb landed a solid punch to Tom's face and more as a result of the ground now becoming wet and slick, Molineaux slipped down to end the round.

Everyone in attendance was treated to an action-packed fifth round. Both fighters landed devastating shots on each other to the head and body. There were several exchanges that lasted over thirty seconds each. Both fighters were giving and taking punishment, thrilling the crowd with the back and forth action. Molineaux avoided a shot that Cribb threw at his head and was able to counter with a hard right to Cribb's left eye, followed by a barrage of punches. Cribb managed to rally back and he feebly threw out and landed a jab to the face of Molineaux, and again, Tom slipped to the ground as the crowd jumped to their feet and cheered. There were NO odds offered at the close of this round.

The sixth round was a short one. Both fighters came towards each other and Molineaux quickly landed a left to Cribb's temple; which sent him down instantly.

During the seventh, Molineaux started out strong, but Cribb rallied and landed a powerful right to the head of Molineaux that sent him backwards, then down to end the round.

Cribb started the eighth fast and was effective landing his punches both to the head and body of Molineaux often, but it had become apparent that Tom Molineaux would not be an easy victory for Cribb. Although the Champion was landing hard, solid punches, Tom was taking them without any trouble. He was certainly not slowing down and began to return Cribb's attack with spirited rallies of his own. When Molineaux landed his punches, Cribb was feeling the effects of Tom's brute strength. Tom Molineaux began to beat up on the Champion with his power shots inside. Cribb was able to move away from the hammering he was receiving from the inside attack of Molineaux and successfully counter-punched, landing several hard shots in a row directly to the face of the black which eventually caused him to go down to a knee to end one of the most exciting, back and forth action-packed rounds of the fight so far.

By the time the ninth round began, both fighters were showing the signs of this extraordinary battle. Cribb's entire head was swollen and becoming disfigured. The top of Molineaux's head was also swollen and blood was flowing freely from both of these warriors. Despite the damage to both fighters, this round continued at a very fast pace. It ended when Molineaux landed a tremendous shot to the face of Cribb, which sent him down. By this time, not much was being done with the odds! Molineaux proved he was no easy win and had the odds makers nervous with the four-to-one odds they had set.

Pierce Egan noted, *"Molineaux gave such proofs of gluttony, that four to one now made many tremble who had sported it."*

As the tenth round began, Molineaux actually started to show signs of tiring, but as the stanza progressed, he was able to rally and battered Cribb around the ring. Molineaux pursued the Champion as if he were his prey. Cribb realized how dangerous an opponent Molineaux was and began to throw punches at Tom while retreating, which was his specialty. The crowd did not know what to think! They were beginning to see that their Champion was being battered and the black was not being affected by Cribb's best shots. As the tenth round continued, both fighters grabbed at each other and fell to the ground simultaneously, ending the round.

Molineaux came out jabbing at the start of the eleventh round. Cribb was comfortable keeping away from the stinging punches that were coming at him from Molineaux. Although most of the punches Molineaux landed were lacking the power he had in the previous rounds, he managed to land a straight shot to the belly of Cribb followed by a tremendous right to the head that sent Cribb down to close out the round.

The twelfth round started with Molineaux attacking Cribb at a furious pace, throwing numerous blows at the Champion, and landing most. Again Tom Cribb found himself moving away from Molineaux's onslaught when he saw an opening and landed a devastating punch to the body of Molineaux. But remarkably, Molineaux shrugged it off and proceeded to land a flurry of punches to the head of Cribb and then threw the Champion to the ground to end the twelfth.

Pierce Egan commented on the body punch and how the round came to an end, *"The Champion put in a severe body blow, but the Moor treated it with indifference, and in return not only milled Cribb's head, but in closing threw him."*

Molineaux charged towards his opponent to start the thirteenth frame. He landed a hard right hand blow to Cribb's head but missed with a clubbing left as the Champion moved away from danger. As Tom lunged inward again hoping to land another power right, Cribb quickly countered with a right of his own that landed squarely on the Black's face. The Champion's punch landed with such force that it even sent him reeling back and down to the ground to end the round, the impact of his own blow having stunned Tom Cribb. By this time, the odds had changed. They were now six-to-four on Molineaux.

As the fourteenth round started, Molineaux charged furiously at Cribb looking to end the bout but Cribb lunged towards his attacker and forced a clinch. As the two men separated, Molineaux landed a powerful shot to the head of Cribb that sent him crashing to the ground to end the round.

The fifteenth was another action-packed, crowd-pleasing stanza! Both fighters landed several meaningful punches to the head and body of each other and then broke apart as the round began. When the two combatants engaged again, Cribb was able to land a paralyzing shot over the guard of Molineaux, which caused the Black to retaliate by launching a furious attack of his own. Neither fighter would give in and the punches were really flying until Cribb was able to land a crushing shot to the throat of Molineaux, sending him down to end the round.

Pierce Eagan describes part of the action during round fifteen, *"Those persons who were fond of viewing milling, might now witness it in perfection; no shifting, but giving and taking were displayed on both sides, till Molineaux was knocked down from a severe hit he received in his throat."*

Tom continued to attack Cribb during the first part of the sixteenth round. He was able to prevent Cribb from moving by cornering him and then landing several left-right combinations. As a matter of fact, Molineaux was throwing so many punches in a short period of time that almost instantly; the seemingly invincible young fighter punched himself out and was visibly tired. The Champion wasted   no time taking advantage of Molineaux's obvious fatigue. Tom Cribb moved into position and was able to send Molineaux to the ground with a less than solidly landing punch to end the round. The current odds were now even.

During the seventeenth, both fighters seemed to have renewed energy and were determined to perform at the highest level. Almost on cue both men attacked each other which created another highly spirited back and forth rally. Both fighters deserve credit for landing extremely powerful punches, but it was Molineaux who landed one of the hardest punches of the contest when he landed a perfectly timed right hand to the chin sending Cribb staggering back. As Molineaux chased his wounded victim across the ring, attempting to finish him off, he slipped in the mud again and as he fell, grabbed onto Cribb and the two crashed to the ground together ending the round. Molineaux managed to do extra damage to the Champion by landing directly on top of him.

The eighteenth round began with yet another furious non-stop exchange from both fighters, which left them in an exhausted state. Cribb forced the action and was able to land a solid body shot but Molineaux responded with a thudding shot to the Champion's forehead, the impact that sent both Cribb and Molineaux down tangled together again to end the round.

By the time the nineteenth began, you could not distinguish the combatants apart from their features! Both fighters were so disfigured and covered in blood and mud that it was virtually impossible to tell them apart. It was astonishing to all those present that this fight was actually still going on. The brutality that was taking place before their eyes had never been witnessed to this degree before. During this round, Molineaux was on the attack as Cribb was retreating backwards trying to land jabs to the face of his aggressive opponent. Molineaux was able to get under Cribb's jab and got him against the ropes into a headlock and began pummeling him in the face. It was not looking good for the Champion, as Molineaux appeared to be putting him away. Because he had him in the headlock, Cribb was not able to fall, which would have ended the round, so Molineaux kept pounding, on his way to certain victory, which would have captured the Title of World Champion. Molineaux continued pummeling Cribb's face, blow after blow after blow.

Pierce Egan describes the horrific scene; *"To distinguish the combatants by their features would have been utterly impossible, so dreadfully were both their faces beaten."*

As Molineaux continued to batter Cribb against the ropes, his hands had gotten tangled in the ropes in such a way that Cribb was not able to break free of Molineaux's grip, nor could his, by now unconscious, body drop to the dirt to end the round. Instead, Cribb was basically a fighter that was being beaten to death. Molineaux continued to bash Cribb's face without any worry of return fire. The fight should have been over and Tom Molineaux declared the winner and NEW Champion. But it was not.

Cribb's corner was complaining about the tangled situation, citing that Cribb was being held in such a way that he was not able to fall down and they wanted to separate the two fighters. But the umpires insisted this could not be done because by rule, one of the fighters had to hit the ground.

Egan writes, *"The hands of Molineaux caught hold of the ropes and held Cribb in such a singular way, that he could neither make a hit or fall down: and while the seconds were discussing the propriety of separating the combatants, which the umpires thought could not be done till one of the men went down……….."*

This is where the first of two travesties took place.

The fans were shocked at what was unfolding before them. A black American was about to win the Championship and they could not let that happen. Almost two hundred spectators charged the ring. Many of them made it past the outer ring area, to the roped off area and attacked Molineaux. They literally pried Tom's hands and fingers to free his grip on Cribb and in the process, broke at least one of his fingers!

Pierce Egan describes the melee, *"About two hundred persons rushed from the outer exterior to the ring, and it is asserted, that if one of the Moor's fingers was not broken, it was much injured by many of them attempting to remove his hands from the ropes: all the time Molineaux was gaining his wind by laying his head on Cribb's breast, and refusing to release his victim as he fibbed away"*.

As soon as he was free, Cribb fell to the ground, out cold. He was carried back to his corner as they worked to revive him. In the meantime, spectators had to be removed and several sections of rope had to be put back in position. By the time order was back in place, the ring cleared and the fight was to continue, many minutes had passed and Cribb had recovered enough to come out for a few seconds to start the twentieth. But the round ended immediately when Molineaux sent Cribb down in a heap from a single shot to his head.

As the twenty-first round began, Cribb was only somewhat coherent but managed to land a meaningful blow to the body, followed by one to the head of Molineaux who clearly began to suffer the effects of the cold and freezing rain that had been falling since the beginning of the contest. Molineaux landed back-to-back shots to the face of Cribb and then the round ended when Cribb was thrown.

The twenty-second round started slow but soon became Tom's, as he was able to batter Cribb with power punches to both the head and body. A devastating shot to Cribb's chin sent him down to end the round.

Both fighters were tired as the twenty-third round began. In order to get some wind to return, both fighters stood toe-to-toe in the center of the ring and sparred, exchanging lighter punches back and forth. Cribb landed a hard punch on the left eye of Molineaux but Tom turned the momentum back in his favor by landing a cracking shot to Cribb's body, sending him down to end the round.

Molineaux started the twenty-fourth round with a lot of energy, once again attacking Cribb with flurries of hard punches. As he had done before during the bout, Molineaux maneuvered Cribb against the ropes and was about to launch another attack, when Cribb grabbed Tom in a much-needed clinch. Molineaux responded by slamming the Champion to the ground, ending the round.

Cribb started off the twenty-fifth by landing a hard shot to Molineaux's left eye, but it did not stop the Black. Again Molineaux attacked and got the better of Cribb. The round ended when Tom landed a hammer blow to the back of Cribb's head.

Molineaux's left eye was swollen shut by the start of the twenty-sixth round so Cribb decided to work Tom's right eye, landing several shots on it. But Molineaux began to show defensive skill of his own as he bounced away from the Champion landing meaningful punches on the go. Molineaux was punishing Cribb again, when the Champion landed a solid shot to the side of Tom's head, sending him down to end the round.

By the time they came out for the twenty-seventh round, both fighters were clearly weak but still continued to fight. The amount of heart and determination displayed by both men was truly amazing. During a clinch, both men fell, ending the round.

By now, the overall consensus from the crowd was, how long could these two men keep fighting? They got their answer as round twenty-eight began and they both did continue, exchanging shots that could have dropped either of them. After both men fired and absorbed what seemed to be an uncountable amount of power punches, Molineaux landed a devastating blow that landed squarely on the face of Cribb, sending him down and out. Again, Cribb was out, and once again, the fight seemed over! Cribb's seconds dragged their unconscious fighter back to the corner in hopes of reviving him enough within the thirty-second time limit so he could at least stand on his own and come out for the twenty-ninth round.

Henry Miles wrote, *"In the 28th round, after the men were carried to their corners, Cribb was so much exhausted that he could not rise from his second's knee at the call of time, which was uttered loudly by Sir Thomas Apreece."*

Egan noted: *"Cribb fell in so an exhausted state from the severe fibbing in which he had received, that the limited time had expired before he was able to renew the contest, and Sir Thomas Apreece yelled, time…… time………time!"*

This is when the second travesty took place.

When referee Sir Thomas Apreece yelled, "Time," Cribb was not able to continue. He yelled it again a second time and then again for a third time. Cribb was still out and for all intents and purposes, Tom Molineaux, by rule should have been declared the winner, right then. But he was not. Cribb was the hometown fighter and to the assembled he looked like the very last English man in the path of the dark-skinned invader. Defeat was unacceptable.

At that moment, one of Cribb's seconds, Joe Ward, leaped into the ring and accused Molineaux of having bullets in his clenched fists. Molineaux and his corner denied this, but Ward insisted, forcing the referee to demand Molineaux open his hands for inspection. After doing so, and finding that Molineaux did not have anything in his hands, Cribb, who had now enjoyed several minutes of extra time to recover, had regained his senses enough to come out for a twenty-ninth round!

But Cribb was still in serious trouble when the twenty-ninth stanza began and it did not take much of a punch from Molineaux, to again send the should-be former Champion to the ground.

The thirtieth round began and Molineaux went after Cribb with all the power left in his body and once again he battered Cribb around the ring. Tom knew that he should have already been declared the winner of this fight, not once, but twice. He wanted to end the fight once and for all and went after the Champion with the intent of doing it now. He attacked Cribb and landed several hard, powerful shots. Then Molineaux landed a savage shot to the head of Cribb and intended to follow it by grabbing the Champion and throwing him to the ground, but in the process Molineaux lost his footing and hit his own head on one of the ring posts, which left him staggering back to his corner in a daze.

Pierce Egan describes his thoughts on the staggering Molineaux, *"Molineaux, in spite of every disadvantage, with a courage and ferocity unequalled, rising superior to exhaustion and fatigue, rallied his adversary with as much resolution as at the commencement of the fight, his nob defying all the milling it had received, and the punishment appeared to have no decisive effect upon it, and contending nobly with Cribb right and left, knocking him away by his hits, and gallantly concluded the round by closing and throwing the Champion.*

The Moor was now convinced that if he did win, he must do it off by hand, as his sight was much impaired."

When the thirty-first round began, Molineaux was still groggy from the fall and Cribb, known for his stamina, was able to land a powerful shot to the challenger's throat, sending him down to end the round.

The thirty-second round saw both men ready to fight again, but simultaneously, without even exchanging a single punch, both fell from exhaustion to end the round. None of the over ten thousand in attendance could believe that any man could take the punishment that these two warriors endured during this contest.

Considering the state of both fighters at the end of round thirty-two, to the absolute astonishment of everyone in attendance, Molineaux blazed out for round thirty-three with a flurry of blows. Molineaux finished with a left to the right eye of Cribb, sending him down to end the frame. But that burst of punches may have taken the very last speck of energy that Tom Molineaux had left.

Both men were tired. Both could barely stand, but both came to scratch and fought toe-to-toe during round thirty-four. By this time, Molineaux was fighting on instinct. Both of his eyes were swollen shut and he was unable to see. He was swinging at the air as if he were blindfolded. Cribb, who was also exhausted, was able to see enough to hit Tom, but without much power. He was able to land several punches while moving away from Molineaux's swinging arms. Cribb landed a multi-punch combination to what was left of Molineaux's face sending him down to end the round. Tom was dragged to his corner by his seconds.

The thirty-fifth round began and ended quickly when Cribb landed a short punch to the head of Molineaux sending him down.

The thirty-sixth saw Molineaux being pointed in the direction of where Cribb was, but as soon as the Black was in range, Cribb popped him in the face, which sent him down.

When the thirty-seventh round began, it appeared that Molineaux may have been getting some energy back as he seemed to move a little faster, however he clearly did not regain his vision as the Champion once again was able to send the challenger down from a punch that had minimum impact.

Both men were done as the thirty-eighth round commenced, and both went down as they clinched.

Barely on their feet to start the thirty-ninth, it did not look like either fighter could last much longer, however Cribb appeared in slightly better shape. Both Molineaux and Cribb were beaten beyond recognition. As Molineaux tried to "feel" his way into position to land a punch, Cribb beat him to it, landing a flurry sending Molineaux down and barely conscious. Once again Richmond had to drag his fighter back to the corner. Tom muttered the words, *"I can fight no more."* But Richmond convinced his fighter to give it one more shot and he agreed. As Molineaux rose to start the fortieth round, he collapsed, unconscious and was not able to continue. He was counted out, giving Tom Cribb the victory. It was forty rounds of brutality that lasted fifty-five minutes and it contained two travesties that would be virtually forgotten by American history.

Pierce Egan wrote, *"At the conclusion of the round, the Moor for the first time complained "He could fight No More!" but his seconds who viewed the nicety of the point, persuaded him to try the chance of another round, to which request   he*

acquiesced, when he fell from weakness, reflecting additional credit on the manhood of his brave conqueror, Tom Cribb."
This fight was the most ferocious and brutal match to have ever taken place up to that time.

Pierce Egan's ringside report included this quote: *"This battle betwixt Cribb and Molineaux was not only more formidable in its nature, but more ferocious and sanguinary. FIFTY FIVE minutes of unprecedented milling before the Moor thought he had had enough!!"*

Egan felt it was the greatest battle he had ever witnessed. The amount of damage each of the combatants inflicted upon each other is almost incomprehensible. The fight lasted for almost one hour. Both fighters had to be carried off and it took several days for each to recover enough to speak.

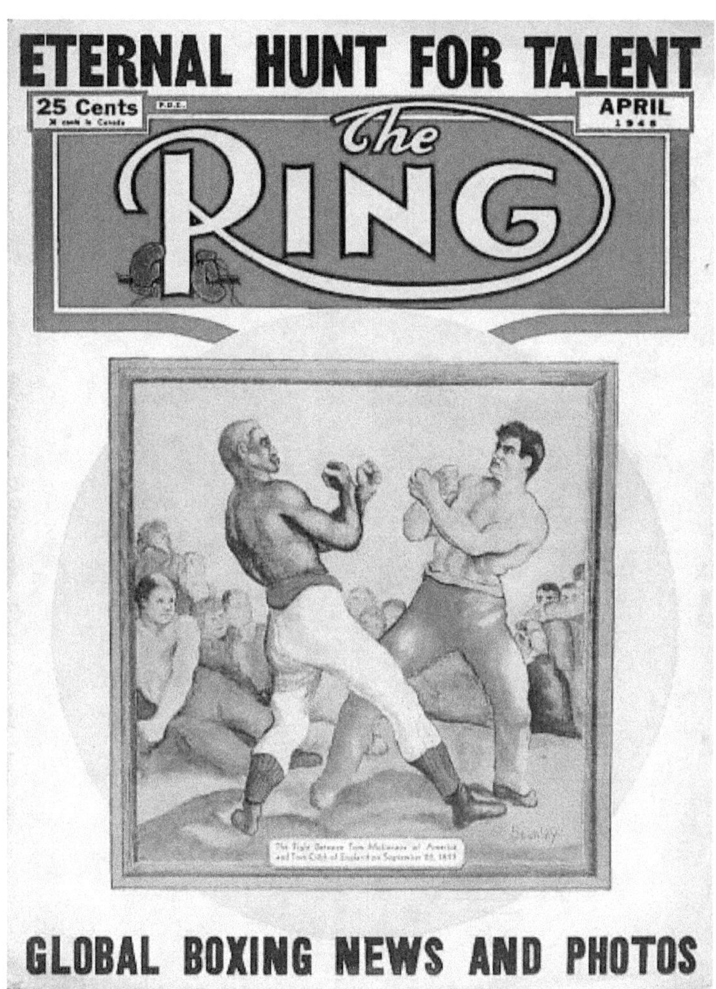
ETERNAL HUNT FOR TALENT
25 Cents
APRIL
1948
The RING
GLOBAL BOXING NEWS AND PHOTOS

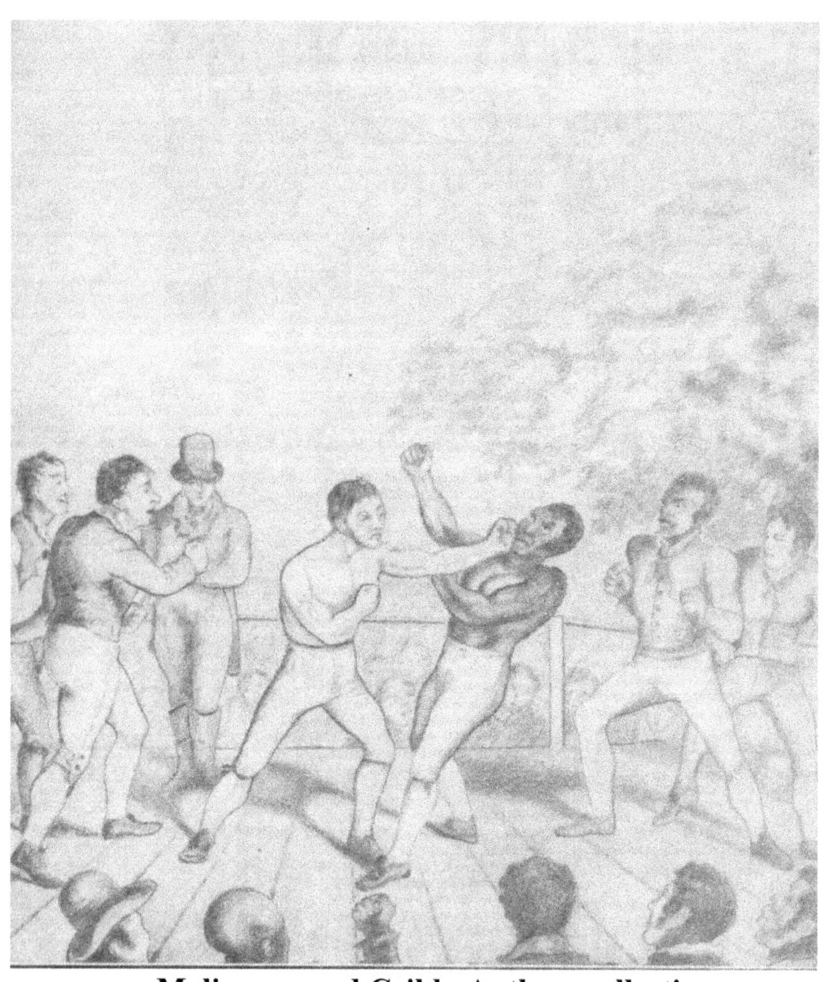

Molineaux and Cribb. Authors collection

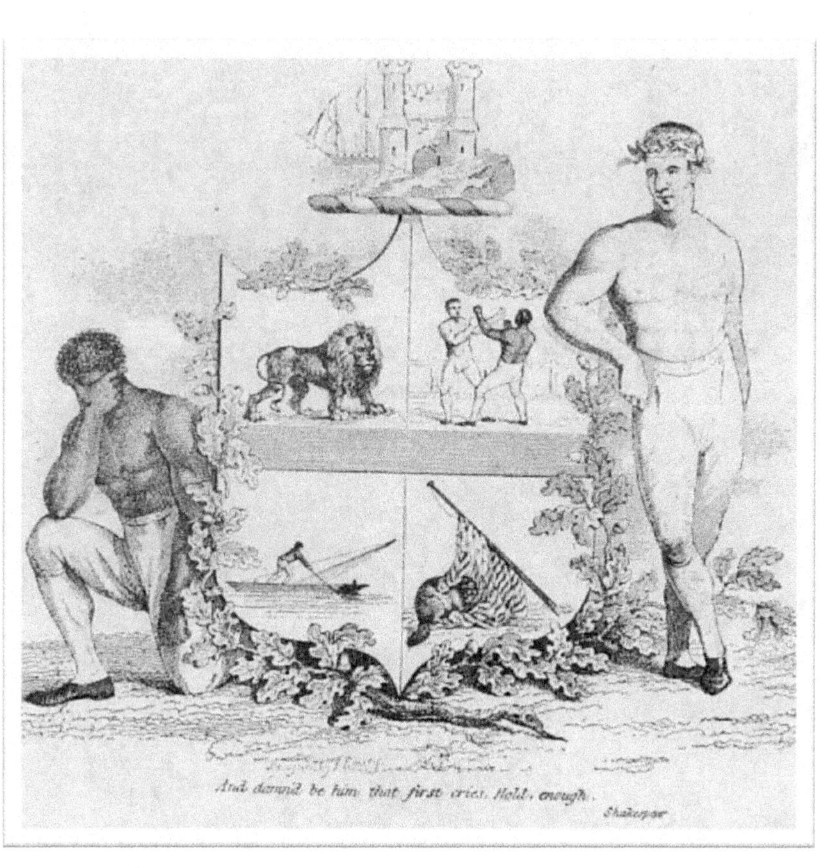
And damn'd be him, that first cries, Hold, enough.
Shakespear

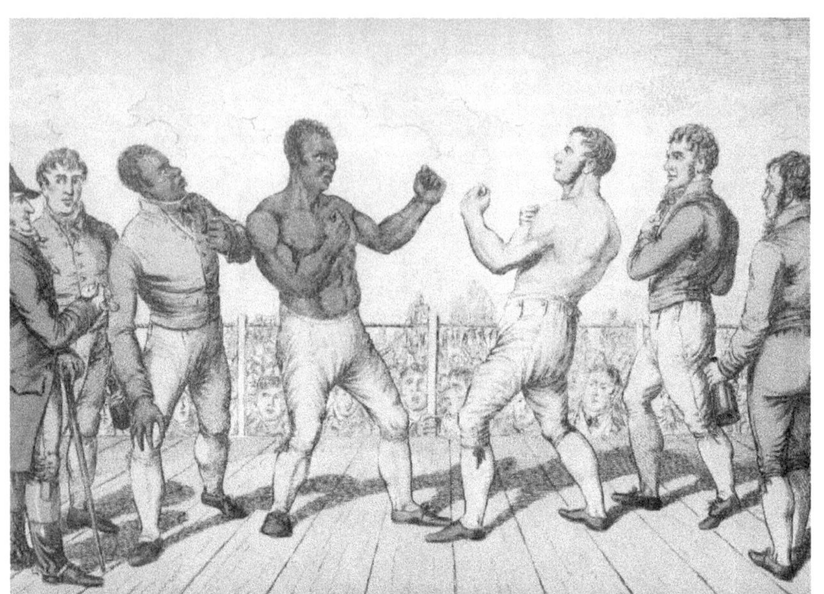

**Molineaux and Cribb September 28, 1811.
Author's collection.**

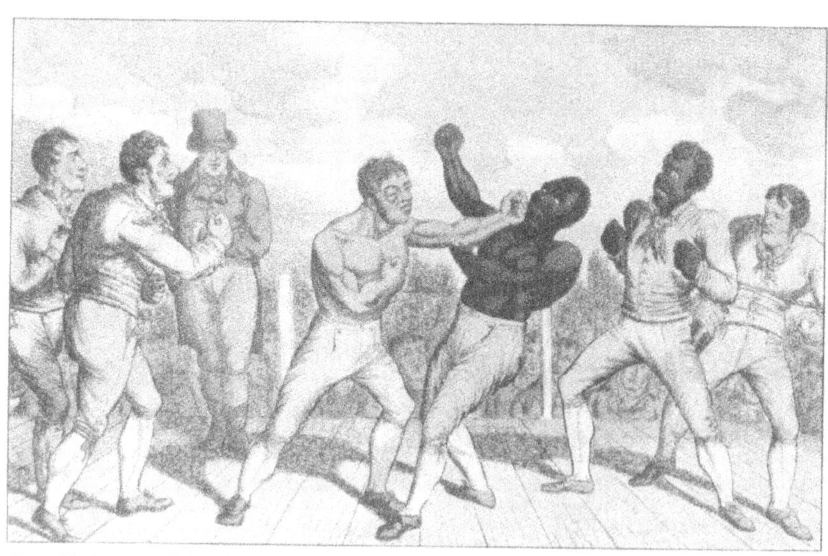

Tom Molineaux fights Tom Crib, 28th September 1811 (print). On 27 July 1812 in Exeter Molineux lost in a wrestling match against John Snow of Moretonhampstead.

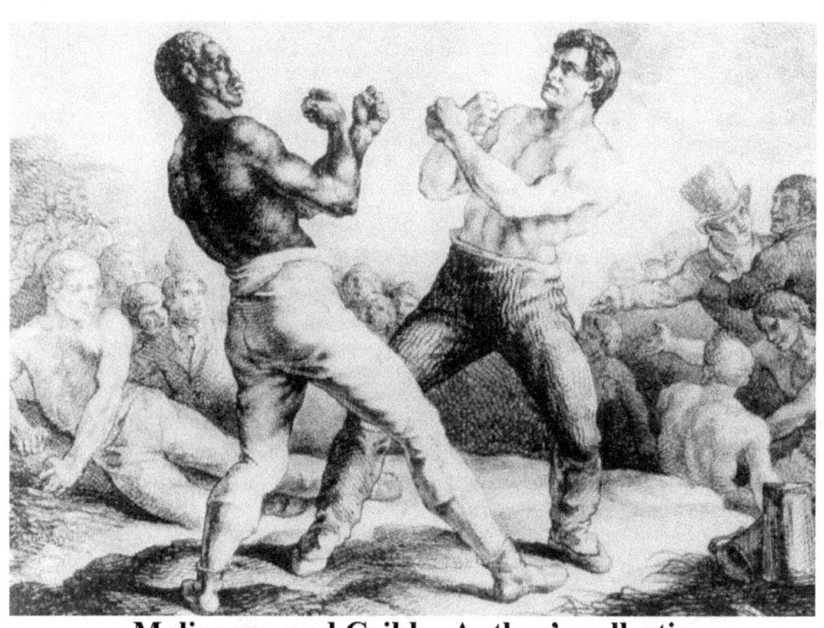

Molineaux and Cribb. Author's collection.

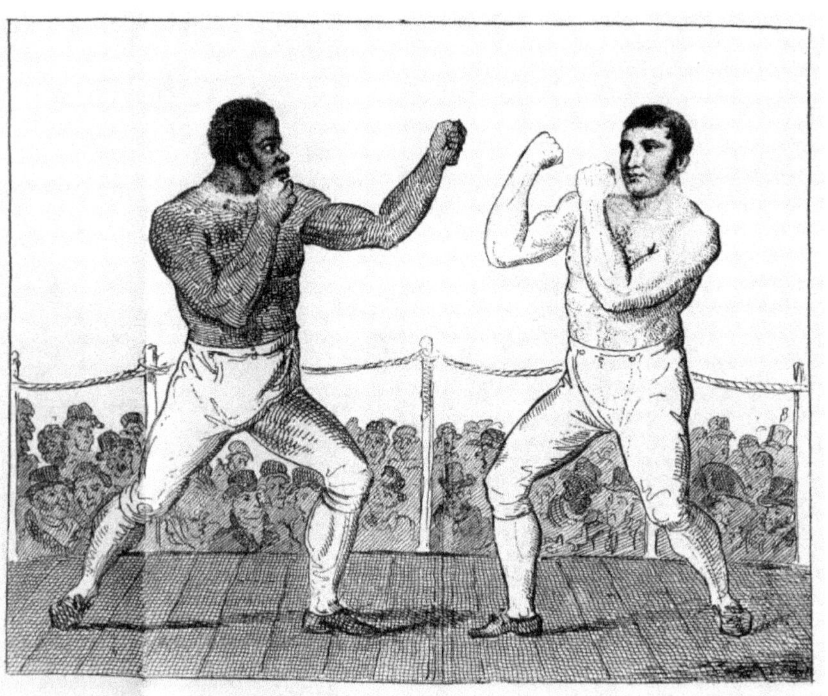

THE SECOND CONTEST BETWEEN CRIB & MOLINEUX, SEPT.28:1811.
Published by Jno.º Smeeton, Dec.r 17, 1812.

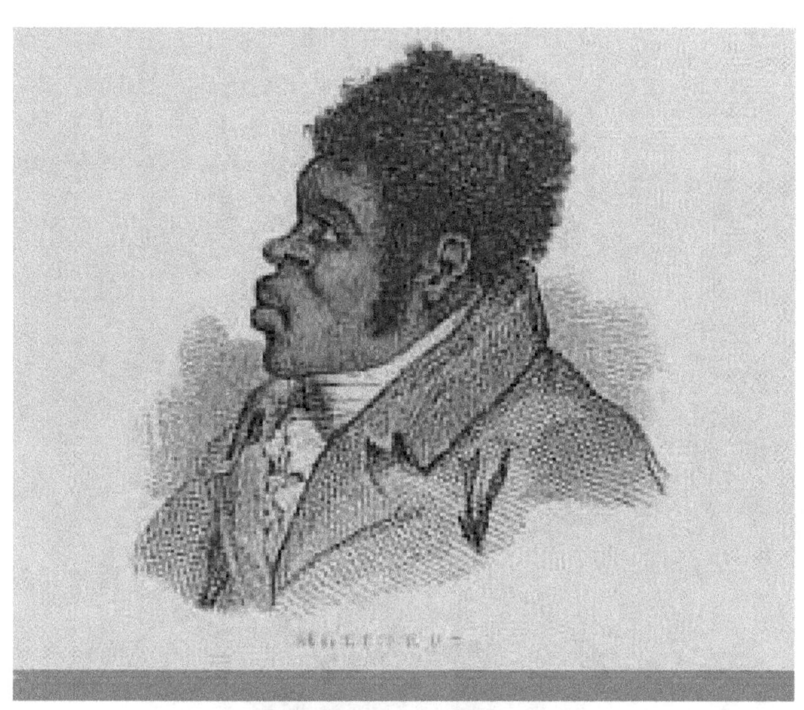

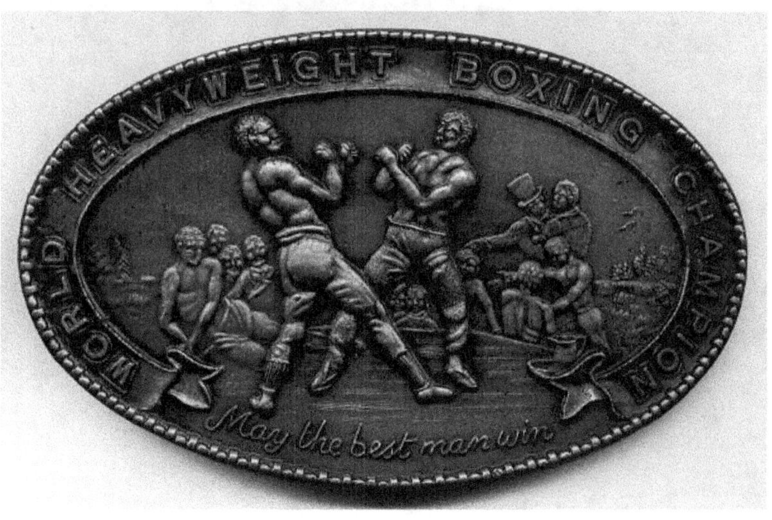

WORLD HEAVYWEIGHT BOXING CHAMPION
May the best man win

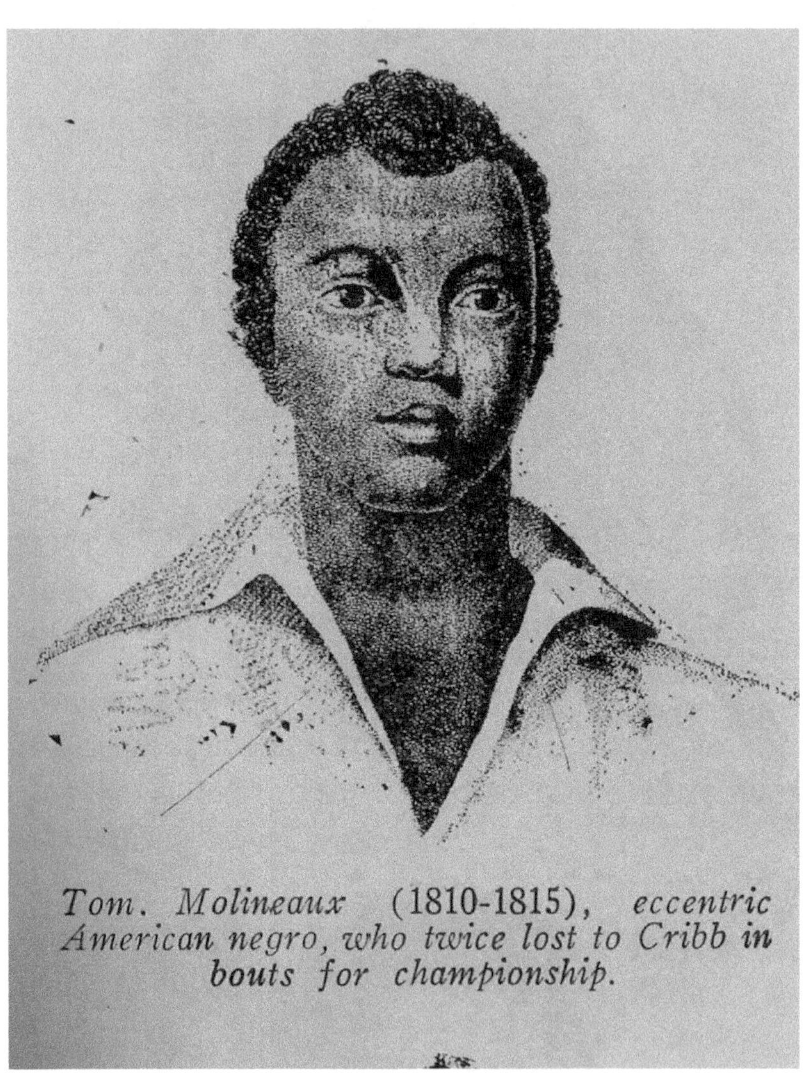

Tom. Molineaux (1810-1815), *eccentric American negro, who twice lost to Cribb in bouts for championship.*

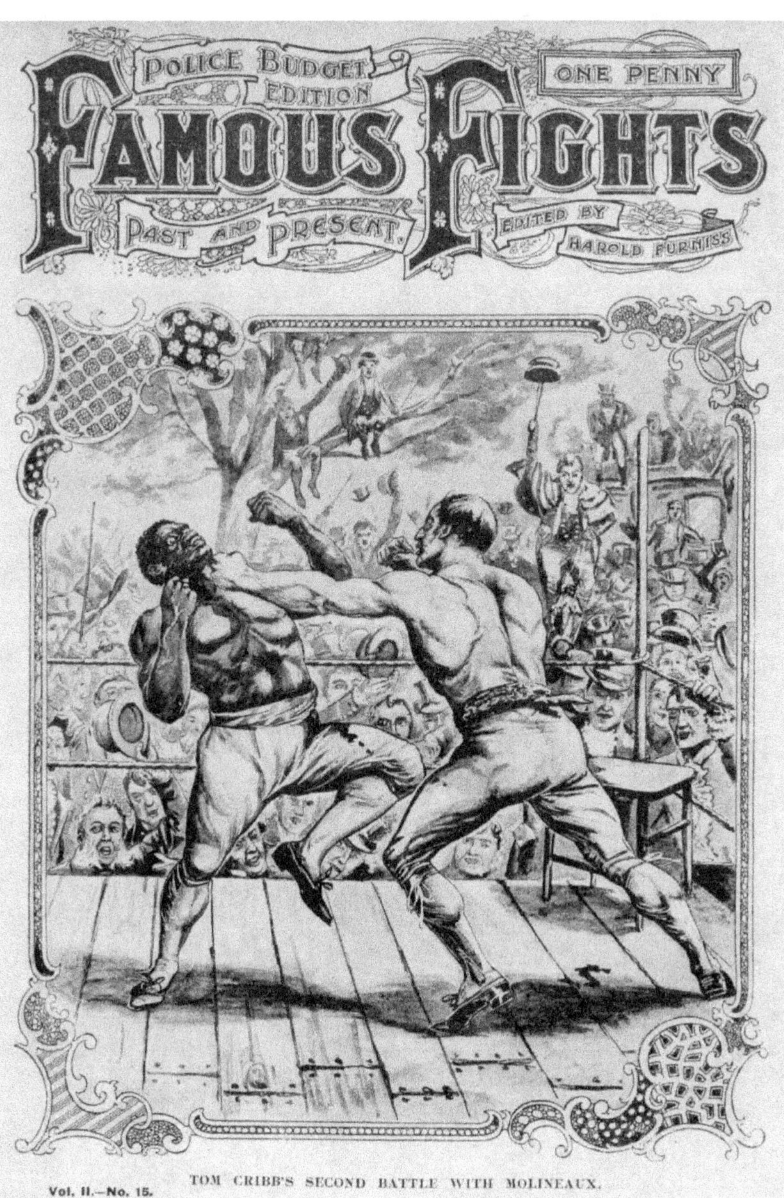

Vol. II.—No. 15.   TOM CRIBB'S SECOND BATTLE WITH MOLINEAUX.

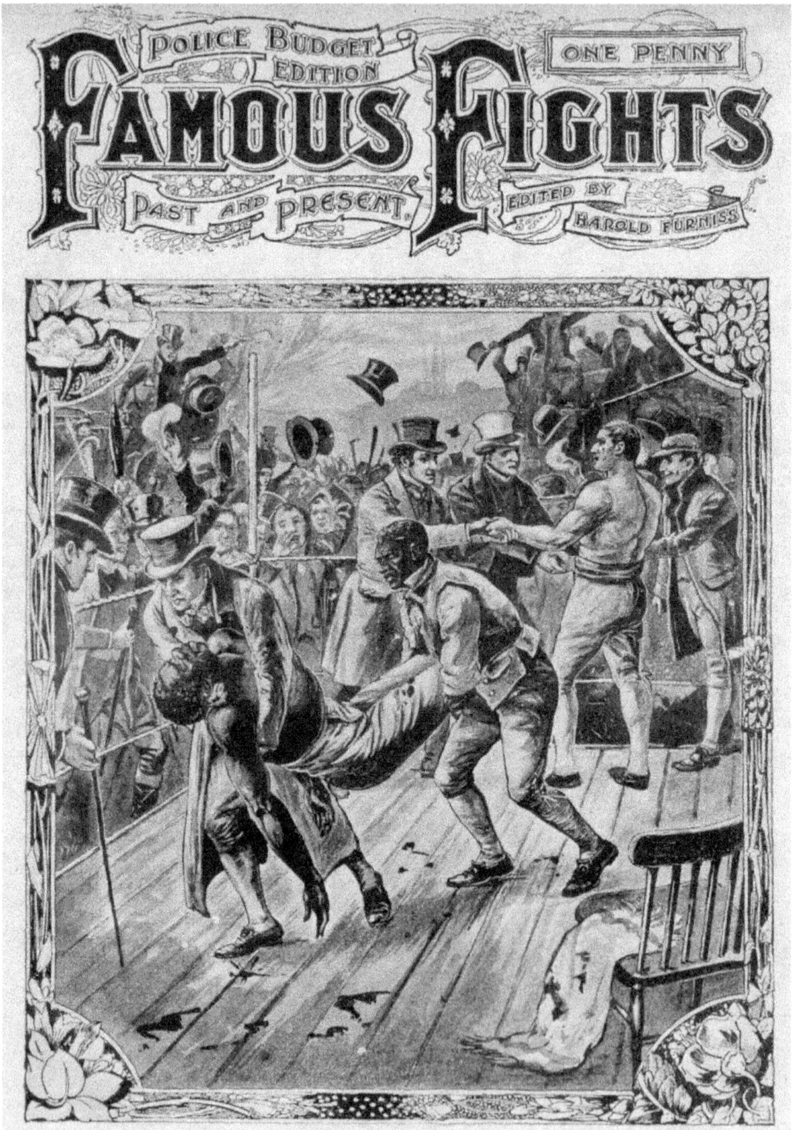

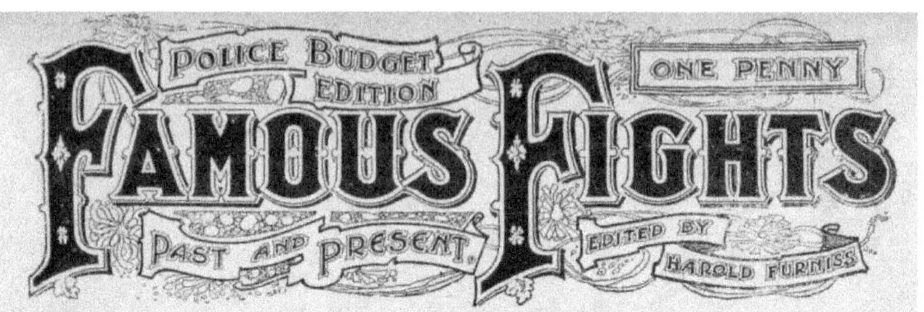

TOM CRIBB'S FIRST DEFEAT OF MOLINEAUX.

80

The English were known, and are still known for being great sportsmen. They pride themselves on being fair. "May the best man win," How ironic is it that the fight between Tom Cribb and Tom Molineaux would end the way it did?

Many people who were in attendance felt that Molineaux lost as a result of foul play and so did Tom himself. Although the pride of England was at stake, the taste of an improper result did not sit well with the majority of boxing fans. As a matter of fact, most that were in attendance, and many who read about the great fight, felt a rematch was in order.

An account of the fight was reported in the December 1810 issue of the "Licensed Vietnallers Gazette." The title of the article said it all; ***"A Blot on the Escutcheon – Cribb and Molineaux – Disgraceful Battle For The Belt."***

The talk of a rematch had begun. Most Englishman felt that Molineaux deserved another shot at Cribb's Title. Some used the hint of foul play, while others justified a rematch based on Molineaux's performance, leaving out the foul play part completely.

No matter how you look at it, the fact is that Tom Molineaux wuz robbed! He was robbed not once, but TWICE. The first was at the point when the spectators charged the combatants and interfered with the fight, preventing Molineaux from securing the victory. Tom Cribb was revived in those valuable minutes while the intervening spectators had to be removed and then order restored before the battle could resume. Even at the start of the twentieth round, Cribb was still basically out on his feet and the round only lasted a few seconds.

The second point at which victory was stolen from Tom Molineaux came at the end of the twenty-eighth round. Once again, Cribb was not able to come to scratch within the thirty-second time limit. He was ordered to fight by the referee yelling TIME, not once, not twice, but three times. Based on the rules, the fight should have been over when Cribb couldn't continue after the first time referee Sir Thomas Apreece yelled TIME and the title awarded to Tom Molineaux. But it was not. Instead one of Cribb's seconds, Joe Ward, ran out and caused a diversion Angelo Dundee would be proud of! He claimed that Tom Molineaux had bullets in his hands. His charge was such a serious one and his insistence was so strong that the referee and both umpires forced Molineaux to open his hands. Upon doing so, no bullets were found. But by this time, Cribb was revived enough to come out to start the twenty-ninth round.

During this era, having fans interfere, or having a second buy himself a few extra moments before a referee called time was common. Make no mistake, these were not legal moves, however it did happen. But the one rule that was enforced, that could be considered sacred, was the thirty-second come- to-scratch rule. If the referee yelled the word time, and a fighter was not able to stand and fight, the contest was over. The fighter who could not fight in the allotted time lost. Case closed.

But Molineaux was robbed of the championship because he was an American, a black American. The English spectators that day would simply not allow Molineaux to win the championship. They helped prevent Molineaux from winning the title because he was black. Fair play? Double standards? In today's world, there would have been far more outrage than a few newspaper articles and tavern talk. Unfortunately for Tom, he lived during a time when he was lucky enough to have a warm place to recover from his battle wounds.

Bill Richmond knew that Molineaux had been deprived of a victory, but he also knew that he had to be very careful of how he approached having Molineaux call out Cribb for a rematch. Richmond had to make sure that Molineaux did not offend anyone that would be in the position of preventing what Richmond knew would be a very profitable rematch. Was Tom Molineaux cheated out of the Heavyweight Title? Of course he was and Bill Richmond knew it, but business was business.

After Molineaux had healed, Bill Richmond helped him publish the following letter in the newspaper:

Pugilistic Challenge To Mr. Tom Cribb

Sir – My friends think that had the weather on last Tuesday, on which I contended with you, not been so unfavorable, I should have won the battle. I therefore challenge you to a second meeting, at anytime within two months, for such a sum as those gentleman who place confidence in me may be pleased to arrange. As it is possible that this letter may meet the public eye, I cannot omit the opportunity of expressing a confident hope that the circumstances of my being of a different color to that of a people amongst whom I have sought protection, will not in any way operate to my prejudice.

I am, sir, your most obedient humble servant, T. Molineaux.
(25)

Tom Cribb was in no hurry to give Molineaux a rematch, despite the huge interest in the bout. The contest had renewed Cribb's popularity. As a matter of fact, it renewed interest in prizefighting. All of a sudden, everyone was talking of the fight, a potential rematch, and that of other young prospects that were coming onto the scene.

Cribb's backers wanted to recognize their hero and champion, so they organized a huge banquet in his honor in January of 1811. It was held at the Fives Court and over three thousand people were in attendance. Tom Molineaux and Bill Richmond were among them. Molineaux wanted to show Cribb, and all that were present, that he had nothing against the Champion, so he sparred with Bill Richmond in honor of his conqueror. They drew a standing ovation when they were done. The whispers among the crowd were that of the rematch. It was Tom Cribb's turn to give his speech. He began thanking everyone, including Molineaux and Richmond. When the crowd asked if Cribb would grant Molineaux a rematch, Cribb said "yes" and the crowd erupted in applause. But when the crowd quieted down enough for Cribb to continue, he said he would only fight Molineaux for 250 guineas per side. Cribb knew that there was no way Richmond and Molineaux could raise that kind of money. Richmond had to stand up and right there in public, explain that they could not raise the money, but they would leave the offer open for twelve months in hopes of raising the capital to make the bout happen. The rematch was inevitable, but Cribb knew that he'd be able to rest up while Molineaux was forced to fight in order to make the stake money. As Richmond was about to sit, he yelled to all, "Tom Molineaux will fight any man alive for 100 pounds per side!"

There weren't too many fighters ready to jump in with Molineaux, but also in attendance that night was Bob Gregson. Bob had been working with a young fighter from Lancashire named Will Rimmer. Will looked very good during his sparring matches that night and Gregson felt that he demonstrated enough skill to compete with Molineaux and accepted Richmond's offer on behalf of Rimmer. It was agreed that Richmond, Molineaux, Rimmer and Gregson would sign the articles at his Castle Tavern the next day.

When Richmond and Molineaux arrived at the Castle Tavern, Bob Gregson was singing a different tune. He refused to pay the agreed upon price of 100 pounds per side and said the fight was only worth fifty-pounds per side. Bill Richmond was livid. He and Gregson almost fought right then, but Bill was able to compose himself enough to leave the Castle Tavern with Molineaux. The fight with Rimmer was off.

Molineaux had become one of the biggest celebrities around. His fame brought fortune, which he continued to spend on spirits, clothes and of course, women. He was not training and began to believe that he did not need to, at all. He believed, beyond any doubt, that he could beat any man alive. As much as Molineaux was enjoying his fame and new life-style, it was not cheap and he soon needed money. Bill Richmond had to find Tom a fight so he could raise money for the Cribb rematch and to support the lifestyle that Molineaux was now enjoying. Luckily for Richmond, the sporting world could not get enough of Tom Molineaux.

On April 2, 1811 Tom Molineaux was given a benefit at the Fives Court where close to twelve hundred people showed up. Molineaux thrilled the crowd by sparring with Tom Belcher, Ben Burn and Isaac Bittoon, three quality prizefighters of the time. Despite their talent level, none could compete with Molineaux. The crowd loved every minute of it, cheering at Tom's every move. When Molineaux was finished for the evening, he left the stage to a standing ovation. Richmond and Molineaux joined the crowd and watched the rest of the sparring matches. Among the fighters was Will Rimmer. To Rimmer's credit, he looked very good and many thought he was a top rate pugilist. They gave so much praise that Bob Gregson became convinced that his young fighter could best Molineaux in a match. He told Richmond that he would put up the one hundred pounds to fight. This time, the articles were signed and the Molineaux-Rimmer fight was to take place in May.

Richmond thought Tom would get back to training, but he was wrong. Molineaux had no desire to train. As a matter of fact, he was becoming very hard to handle for Richmond. Every time Bill attempted to instruct Molineaux on how to train, or what he should be doing, etc, Molineaux would threaten to leave him for another trainer and manager. Richmond was not about to lose Molineaux now when he was about to make some real money, so rather than direct Molineaux on the right path, he gave in and let Tom run wild with the women and the spirits. As the days turned to weeks, Molineaux continued to party and training was the furthest thing from his mind.

The Molineaux-Rimmer contest took place at Moulsey Hurst on May 21, 1811. It had been almost six months since the Cribb fight and the demand for Tom Molineaux was unbelievable. There were over 10,000 fans in attendance t o see Molineaux in his first set-to since his controversial loss to Cribb.

Rimmer was a big man and was almost twenty-three years old. He had several prior fights, but none of his opponents had the skill of Tom Molineaux. The battle area was a twenty-five foot roped-off ring. Rimmer was seconded by Powers and Jones and Gregson as his backer. Richmond and Bill Gibbons seconded Molineaux. Before the start of the contest the odds were in favor of Molineaux at three-to-one.

The first round started off with the two fighters sparring toe-to-toe for a little over two minutes. Rimmer tried to step-up the pace when he threw a hard right-left combo, but his lack of experience showed when his distance was off enough to enable Molineaux to counter punch with such a devastating right to Rimmer's neck, it knocked him off his feet to end the stanza.

Rimmer came out fast and furious at the start of the second, throwing a right followed by a left that grazed Molineaux.

Again he was off on his distance, which enabled Molineaux to defend Rimmer's attack easily. Both fighters engaged and worked at each other inside until Molineaux pushed Rimmer off and then unleashed a barrage of power shots that put the Lancashire man in trouble. A solid right-left combo sent Rimmer down to end the round.

Pierce Egan describes the second: "The Black's powers were witnessed, he punished Rimmer in a dreadful style, and knocked him down, by tremendous blows right and left, with uncommon celerity and science."

Molineaux was extremely confident going into round three. He began grinning and clowning by crouching down very low, showing little respect towards Rimmer. Molineaux was daring Rimmer to throw a punch, which he finally did, and almost effortlessly Tom avoided Rimmer's blow and counter- punched with a flurry of hard, powerful shots that battered Rimmer so badly the Lancashire tough fell to his knees purposely just to avoid more blows.

As the fourth round began, Rimmer's face and head were becoming disfigured before ten thousand pairs of eyes. The impact of Molineaux's punches was doing irreversible damage to Rimmer's appearance. Molineaux continued to batter his foe with flurries of punches until he landed a picture perfect left-right combo to the head of Rimmer, which sent him down, as Egan described in his report, "as if he were shot." The crowd roared its approval for Tom Molineaux as he headed to his corner.

The fifth and sixth rounds were carbon copies of each other. Rimmer was beaten, tired, and about to go and went down to end both rounds virtually on his own as Molineaux clowned once again.

The seventh may have been Rimmer's best. He rallied to the point where he was getting the better of Molineaux as they exchanged bombs, toe-to-toe in the center of the ring. Molineaux was forced to clinch and in doing so, tangled his legs with Rimmer's sending both combatants to the turf to end the round.

The eighth saw Rimmer charge Molineaux and throw him down to end the round. Molineaux was visibly upset with this. He stormed back to his corner huffing and puffing like a bull.

As the ninth began, Molineaux attacked Rimmer with a frenzy of vicious blows that battered the man from Lancashire around the ring like a pinball. Rimmer's face looked like hamburger as a paralyzing right from Molineaux connected with the force of a sledgehammer to send him face down in the dirt to end the beating and the round.

Shockingly, Rimmer was full of vigor as the tenth round started. He seemed like a new man. He was able to exchange a few shots with Molineaux and was beginning to rally when his lack of experience betrayed him again as he misjudged the distance of a would-be power shot that missed its target. Rimmer was able to force a clinch and the two men wrestled each other to the ground to end the stanza.

The eleventh, twelfth and thirteenth rounds were uneventful. Rimmer was a beaten man. He could hardly stand and was taking a serious beating. His features were permanently altered, he was bleeding profusely and he could hardly get in a full breath of air. Tom Molineaux was toying with his opponent as a cat would toy with a dying mouse.

Rimmer was a finished fighter, but he refused to quit. He tried to get some wind by running around the ring to start the first few minutes of the fourteenth frame, but Molineaux was not willing to let the charade continue. He cut off the ring and cornered Rimmer and when in the correct position, Molineaux landed an atomic left-right-left combo to the gut of his opponent, sending him down to end the round.

As Molineaux returned to his corner, Rimmer remained face down in the ring. At that moment, the ropes were broken and the ring charged by several spectators. Apparently, they had become agitated that a black man was beating an Englishman so savagely and effortlessly. Before order was restored, and the ropes put back in place, twenty-minutes had passed. The fight continued but despite every possible effort by his seconds, backers and even his supporters in the crowd, Rimmer was a beaten fighter, and more importantly, a beaten man. The one-sided affair continued on for six more rounds until the game Rimmer was unconscious and was not able to continue to start the twenty-first round, giving Tom Molineaux a triumphant victory.

Molineaux's one-sided destruction of Will Rimmer added even more firepower to the argument that many believed, whether they liked it or not, that Tom was an exceptional fighter and would likely be Champion if not for the foul play in his first match with Cribb. There was no doubt about it now; there was only one fight that had to be made: Cribb vs. Molineaux II.

Chapter 7

Tom Molineaux had become a household name. The talk of a rematch between Molineaux and Cribb was the main topic of discussion throughout London. But Tom Cribb was refusing to entertain any talk of a rematch until Molineaux and Richmond were able to put up the two hundred fifty guineas that he demanded, if it was even possible. As a matter of fact, Cribb stated publicly that he was so confident that Molineaux would not be able to obtain the appropriate backing, that he was again officially retired. Cribb enjoyed drinking to his retirement with his friends. He had a lot of friends, which meant lots of ale for the retired Champion.

Since his controversial loss to the Champion of England and after his brutal victory over Rimmer, Molineaux wasn't able to find opponents willing to get into the ring with him. How would Molineaux and Richmond raise the funds needed to secure a rematch with Cribb if there were no willing opponents?

Bill Richmond had the answer. He instructed Tom that while he was out on the town, he needed to make sure and talk about his intentions. If Cribb would not grant him a rematch, and there were no others willing to get into the ring with him, then Molineaux would simply claim the Champion of England Title. Soon the press began printing Molineaux's statements and the desire for a rematch became even greater. The talk was in fearful tones; Cribb had to agree to the rematch soon because once again, the honor of England was at stake. The Championship cannot fall into the hands of a foreigner…an American…especially a black one.

Pierce Egan wrote: *"The Black had to contend against a prejudiced multitude; the pugilistic honour of the country was*

90

at stake, and the attempts of Molineaux were viewed with jealousy, envy and disgust ~ the national laurels to be borne away by a foreigner ~ the mere idea to an English breast was afflicting, and the reality could not be endured: that it should seem, the spectators were ready to exclaim" ~ "Forbid it heaven, forbid it man!"

By the end of June, Cribb's manager and trainer, Captain Robert Barclay became extremely agitated over this situation. He went to the pub and spoke directly to Cribb and urged him to do what he needed to do to, and for the honor of England, agree to fight Tom Molineaux again. Finally, Cribb responded. "To prevent the Championship of England to be held by a foreigner, I will once again, come out of retirement and fight Tom Molineaux," Cribb proclaimed.

A few days later a meeting took place at Richmond's Horse and Dolphin. In attendance were Tom Molineaux, Bill Richmond, Captain Barclay, Tom Cribb and acting as overseer of the negotiations, John Jackson. Jackson drew up the articles of the contest and collected a new agreed upon amount of three hundred guineas per side. Barclay, who was a very wealthy man, put up the money for the contest. He covered the 300 guineas for Cribb, and Barclay loaned Bill Richmond 300 guineas to put up for Molineaux, which he did, except he had it listed on record as a loan to Molineaux from Richmond, for the purpose of Tom's put-up stake money to fight Cribb a second time. Once again, Cribb insisted the fight be scheduled further in the future than Richmond wanted, setting the fight to take place in September. Cribb knew he had to be in the absolute best shape of his career and this time, Captain Barclay would be in charge of his training camp.

Barclay was no stranger to prizefighting or fitness, as he had once won a bet that he was able to walk one thousand miles in one thousand hours. Many regarded Captain Barclay as one of the greatest sportsmen of the time and Barclay convinced

Cribb to come to his own estate at Ury and begin his training for the second Molineaux encounter. Cribb agreed and arrived at the estate on July 7, 1811.

Long term training regiments for prizefighting were rare during the time. But Barclay was an advocate for strict training procedures, which included diet and exercise. He would keep detailed records, in writing, of the entire training process. Captain Barclay recorded Cribb's progress from the time he arrived at Ury through the time he was ready to leave.

Captain Barclay's complete hand-written account of Cribb's training camp, as he prepared for his second fight with Molineaux, read as follows: –*The Champion arrived on the 7th of July 1811, he weighed sixteen stone, and from his mode of living in London and the confinement of a crowded city, he had become corpulent, big-bellied, full of gross humors and short breathed, and it was with difficulty he could walk ten miles. He first went through a course of physic, which consisted of three doses, but for two weeks he walked about as he pleased and generally traversed the woods and plantations with a fowling piece in his hand.*

The reports of his gun resounded everywhere through the groves and the hollows of that delightful place, to the great terror of the magpies and wood pigeons. After amusing himself in this way for about a fortnight, he then commenced his regular walking exercise, which at first was about ten or twelve miles a day. It was soon after increased to eighteen or twenty and he ran regularly morning and evening a quarter of a mile at the top of his speed.

In consequence of his physic and exercise, his weight was reduced in the course of five weeks, from sixteen stone to fourteen and nine pounds, at this period he commenced his sweats, and took three during the month he remained at Ury afterwards, and his weight was gradually reduced to   thirteen

By the time Cribb left Ury and Barclay's training camp, the Champion felt he was in the best shape of his life. Cribb   was extremely confident that this second time he would no doubt, conquer "The Terrible Black" as Molineaux was now being called, and restore confidence that the Championship would remain in its rightful place, England.

Molineaux's training camp was nothing at all like Cribb's because there wasn't a Tom Molineaux training camp. Molineaux's arrogance was at an all-time high. He enjoyed traveling, dressing in fancy clothes, and drinking and whoring around in excess. Even his closest supporters were getting angry at Tom's attitude and lack of commitment. He had not entered the gym, nor was he training at all. He was often heard arguing with Richmond and at times, it seemed the two would come to blows, or at the very least, part ways.

But Richmond saw this building up for the past six months, since the first meeting with Cribb in December of 1810. It was the reason the stake money for the second Cribb fight was recorded as a loan from Richmond to Molineaux. The result was that payments had to be made and the only way Tom could raise the money to pay Richmond was to fight.

Since Molineaux was such a big attraction, Richmond decided to take him on a tour to fight exhibitions in order to raise money for training expenses, and so that Tom could begin paying Bill back for the stake money. So Richmond, Molineaux and Tom Belcher, the brother of Jem Belcher, began touring the provinces putting on prizefighting exhibitions. The tour was a financial success. Midway through the schedule, Molineaux had become quite the breadwinner and Bill Richmond was benefiting from it, big time, in his wallet.

About two weeks prior to the scheduled contest, Richmond ended the tour and the men returned to the Horse and Dolphin. Molineaux looked to be in great shape, as his muscles would glisten in the sun, but as a result of his late-night life style,   he was not in the real fighting-shape he should have been in to go up against Tom Cribb, who was at his very best. Despite his complete lack of training, Tom was still very confident that he would not only win, but he would win easily.

The rematch was the biggest event that boxing had ever seen to date. Not only was the anticipation coming from the sporting world, it was also the main interest and topic of discussion for most Englishmen from all walks of life. By today's standards, it was greater than some of the sport's most famous match-ups including Ali-Frazier, Johnson-Jeffries, Hagler-Leonard and Holmes-Cooney.

On the morning of the contest, Pierce Egan gives us a picture of what was on most Englishmen's minds: *"Whether Old England still should retain her proud characteristic of conquering; or that an American, and a man of colour, should win the honour, wear it, and carry it away from the shores of Britain. Never was the sporting world so much interested."*

The contest took place at Thistleton Gap on September 28, 1811. For over a week leading up to the fight, there wasn't a bed, a spot on the floor, in a barn, or even on the grass for anyone to sleep within miles of the fight site. Over 20,000 people were in attendance by noontime and the surrounding areas were mobbed with boxing fans trying to get there. The crowd didn't just include members of The Fancy. There were many nobles and men who were regarded as being of great importance or influence in attendance as well. Some of the more famous people of the time that were documented as being present for the highly anticipated rematch were General Grosvenor, Lord Yarmouth, the Honorable Berkeley Craven, Lord Pomfret, Sir Henry Smyth, Sir Charles Alton, Sir Francis Baynton, Major Mellish, Captain Barclay, Thomas Goddard, Mr. Gore & co. and the Marquis of Queensbury. The fans came by foot, horse and in wheeled vehicles from the most luxurious of the era down to common wagons and donkey carts.

Cribb looked to be and was in top shape, and although Molineaux looked like he was, truth be told, he was not. For the past several months, he balked at training and was turned loose to do as he pleased. He had taken Cribb so lightly, it had been reported that that just prior to making his way to the location of the contest, Molineaux ate an entire boiled fowl and an apple tart that he washed down with a large tankard of porter for his breakfast.

All accounts of this fight during the time stated that it was by far the largest sporting event to have ever taken place. Fans had begun as early as 6:00 a.m. to make their way to the fight location to get the choice spots. The ring was erected on a twenty-five foot stage placed in a field. It was surrounded by a roped circle, which was used as an outer ring to separate the combatants from the crowd. Beyond the outer ring, the spectators that occupied the front rows, laid down on their sides, while those in the rows behind them, sat on their knees. Outside of the fans kneeling, were hundreds of horsemen and behind them were all of the vehicles. In addition to the twenty thousand present, as the two warriors approached the ring, estimates suggested thousands more who were still trying to make their way to the contest.

Cribb was the first to enter the ring and as Egan wrote, *"to an applause that exceeded everything of its kind."* Molineaux quickly followed Cribb and jumped onto the ring platform and bowed to the crowd as Egan described their reaction, *"The Moor was greeted with tokens of approbation, though not of so general a nature."*

Molineaux seemed on edge as he paced back and forth. Cribb on the other hand, had a very confident look on his face. When the two fighters stripped to prepare for battle, the crowd went crazy. Egan wrote: *"On stripping, the anxiety of the multitude cannot be described; and they were soon brought to the mark by their seconds."*

Tom Cribb was seconded by John Gulley and Joe Ward, while Richmond and Bill Gibbons were in Molineaux's corner. The odds to win the contest were in Cribb's favor at three-to-one and he was also the favorite to draw first blood prior to the start of the bout.

Both fighters met in the center of the ring staring at each other with thoughts of destruction as they shook hands and returned to their corners. The fight began at 12:18p.m. when the referee yelled, "TIME."

The fight started out with Molineaux dominating, as the two pugilists sparred for over a full minute in the center of the ring. Molineaux was landing the more powerful blows of the two, as they found Cribb's face and head. Cribb landed a solid body shot that caused Molineaux to step up his pace, throwing a flurry of punches and connecting solidly with most. Cribb was forced to retreat as Molineaux continued his attack. Molineaux was getting the better of the Champion, until Cribb landed a blow to Molineaux's throat, sending him down to end the round.

Egan describes the blow that ended the round, *"Molineaux received a hit in his throat, which sent him down, though not considered clean."*

The second started with Molineaux landing several powerful left-right combinations to the face and head of Cribb and soon Cribb was bleeding in several places. Molineaux had drawn first blood although most of the betting had gone in Cribb's favor to do so. Cribb tried to retaliate by landing a quick left-right to Molineaux's head, followed by a devastating body shot, which backed the American up. Molineaux then launched an attack of his own, landing several hard shots to Cribb's head, which resulted in the two warriors going toe-to-toe, exchanging bombs in the center of the ring. The action was intense and soon both men clinched and, Molineaux threw Cribb down onto the platform to end the round. The odds now were five-to-two in favor of Cribb.

As the third stanza began, Cribb was already showing the effects of Molineaux's power. His right eye was almost swollen shut and he was bleeding in several places. Molineaux worked Cribb's eye exclusively, as Cribb concentrated on Molineaux's mid-section. Molineaux seemed to crank it up a notch as his punch output increased, until he threw Cribb down to end the round. The odds went to seven-to-four in favor of the Champion.

It's interesting to note Pierce Eagan's report of the third round: "In the last rally the right eye of Cribb was almost darkened; and another now commenced equally as ferocious, after sparring to obtain wind, in which it was perceived the Moor was defective, when the Champion put in a most tremendous doubler in the body of Molineaux, and who, notwithstanding he was hit away, to the astonishment of everyone, renewed the rally in that determined manner, as to create considerable agitation among those persons who had betted the odds. There was a marked difference in their mode of fighting; Cribb hit right and left at the head and body, while the Moor aimed at the nob alone, and with much judgment planted several dexterous flush hits, that impaired the eyesight of Cribb, and his mouth bled considerably. This rally continued a minute and a half, and in closing, the Champion received a heavy fall. The superiority of the Moor's strength was evinced by his grasping the body of Cribb with one hand, and supporting himself by the other resting on the stage; and in this situation threw Cribb completely over upon the stage."

When the fourth started, Molineaux was huffing and puffing, as his utter lack of preparation for the fight of his life began to be exposed. Despite bleeding profusely, Cribb smiled with confidence as he continued to work the body of Tom Molineaux. The challenger rallied with a barrage of solid shots to the head of Cribb, which he was unable to answer, eventually being dropped onto the wooden platform to end the round. The odds did not change, seven-to-four in favor of the Champion.

The fifth started when Molineaux jumped all over Cribb, landing many shots to the head. But Cribb was not done, as he returned the favor and the two exchanged extremely powerful shots in the center of the ring. Molineaux got the better of Cribb and landed a paralyzing right and as the Champion was falling to the floor, Molineaux landed another to end the round.

Eagan describes the action during the fifth round: *"The punishment was truly dreadful on both sides; but the Moor had the best of it, and the Champion fell from a hit, and received another in the act of falling, which occasioned some difference of opinion, but the umpires decided it to be correct, as the hands of Cribb were at Liberty."*

When the sixth began, Molineaux was still having a hard time finding enough air to fill his lungs due to his failure to prepare himself for this contest. In attempt to gain his wind, he t r i e d to move around the ring. But Cribb was too experienced to let his foe off the hook. He followed Molineaux and was able to land a body shot that all but put Molineaux down. The result of the punch had Molineaux desperately trying to breathe and he was not sure what to do to regain his composure. Cribb successfully got into position to throw and land a punch that sent Molineaux down with a crash to end the round. The odds now were five-to-one in favor of Tom Cribb.

Eagan describes the body shot and what transpired to end the stanza: *"Cribb gave the Moor so severe a blow in the body with his right hand, that not only appeared to roll him up, but seemed as if he had completely knocked the wind out of him, which issued so strong from his mouth like smoke from a pipe, that he was literally gasping for breath. On renewing the rally, he behaved quite frantic, and seemed bewildered as to what manner he should conduct himself ~ afraid of his opponent's punishment, he dared not go in, although wishing to do so, and capered about in an extravagant manner, to the derision of Cribb and the spectators, hit short and was quite abroad; when the Champion pursued him around the stage with great success, and concluded the round by a full length hit, which laid the Moor prostrate."*

The seventh started with Molineaux charging Cribb in an attempt at landing the knockout blow and in doing so, he scored with several hard shots to the head of the Champion. But Cribb was in the best shape of his life and Molineaux had not only failed to train, he also could have been suffering from the beginning stages of consumption as a result of his life style, which added to his exhausted state against Cribb. Molineaux was just not able to send Cribb down from his attack; and in response the Champion landed several hard blows to the challenger's neck, which when combined with Molineaux's lack of wind, sent the American to the floor to end the round.

By the time the eighth started, Molineaux was in desperation mode. He could hardly breathe and as he tried to start a rally, found that his distance was not correct and his punches fell short. Cribb capitalized on this and unleashed a flurry of left-right combinations to the head of the Challenger. Molineaux tried to cover up, but Cribb was able to get Molineaux's head locked under his arm and proceeded to pummel away at his face until Molineaux's limp body dropped to the floor ending the round.

100

The ninth was the beginning of the end for Molineaux. He was not able to do much at this point, as his wind was gone, and he was so physically spent that he had lost most of his punching power. Molineaux could no longer keep his h a n d s up high enough to protect himself and Cribb landed a left that had more force than a mule's kick, which upon impact, broke Molineaux's jaw and sent him down in a heap. Richmond and Gibbons had to drag their fighter back to the corner to try to revive him.

Pierce Eagan had an interesting description of this round in his ringside report: *It was so evident which way the battle would now terminate, that it was* **"Lombard Street to a China Orange,"** *Cribb was the conqueror. The Moor in running in, had his jaw broke, and fell as if dead from a tremendous left- handed blow of the Champion."*

When the referee called TIME, Molineaux was not able to continue. But Cribb insisted that he give his black American challenger more time to recover so he could prove once and for all, beyond any shadow of a doubt, in front of all the fans in attendance, who the superior fighter was. And after an extra minute, Molineaux came out for the tenth, showing plenty of heart but he only took more of a beating and was dropped to end the round.

Once more, Cribb allowed Molineaux extra time to make it out for an eleventh round. But Molineaux was a beaten man, as he could hardly stand erect. It only took a few m o r e punches to knock Molineaux out cold. As Tom Molineaux lay unconscious, Cribb danced around his fallen foe, mocking the beaten fighter to the deafening applause from the crowd. The contest was over and once again, Tom Cribb was the victor and still the Champion. The total time of the contest was nineteen minutes and ten seconds.

Eagan describes the reaction of the crowd at the conclusion of the contest: "Such a noise arose, as the shrouds make at sea in a stiff tempest, as loud, and to as many tunes. Hats, cloaks, doublets, I think, flew up; and had their faces been loose, this day they had been lost. Such joy I never saw before."

Eagan continues, *"It appeared in the above battle, that the Moor had acquired science equal to the Champion, and was viewed as a good in-fighter; remarkably quick and weighty with his left hand, and who returned on his opponent's head, whenever he received in the body: but no question now remains concerning the superiority of the combatants ~ Cribb having won a main, and beat the Moor in nineteen minutes and ten seconds, when in the former battle it continued thrice the duration; which can only be accounted for, that Cribb was too full of flesh in that combat, and not in good condition; and Molineaux had improved respecting science, but injured his stamina. The hardiest frame could not resist the blows of the Champion; and it is astonishing the Moor stood them so long. He was taken out of the ring senseless, and could not articulate; and it was thought upon the first examination that his jaw-bone and two of his ribs were fractured; while, on the contrary, Cribb scarcely received a body blow, but his head was terribly out of shape."*

London was ecstatic over the result of this fight. That night an immense crowd assembled in front of Richmond's Horse and Dolphin, the Pad and Swimmer and in Leicester Square to hear all about the battle. Every street in the world's biggest city at the time was blocked. Every tavern and boarding house was filled to its capacity. Things got so crazy that many peace officers were called in to maintain order.

As a result of the Cribb-Molineaux II encounter, several towns had gained considerable attention and grew substantially, especially Grantham and Stamford. England was changed forever as a result of the interest in this match-up.

Tom Cribb was a hero. According to reports, Cribb made 400 pounds for the fight. Captain Barclay made over 10,000 pounds. Many people bet all they had on Cribb. A baker in Borough put up all of his personal property and his house on Cribb and was rewarded with profits that exceeded 1700 pounds. There were even reports of one bet that paid a complete suit of clothes, a walking stick, gloves and a guinea in the pocket.

Molineaux was to make not a penny for his efforts until John Jackson took up a collection and raised fifty-pounds for the game American challenger.

A dinner was held in Tom Cribb's honor for his victory over Molineaux on December 2, 1811 at the Castle Tavern in Holborn. He was presented with a Sliver Cup, which was filled with eighty guineas for his accomplishment and for preventing a foreigner from triumphing over the heroes of England. The cup was engraved with the title Cribb had solidified as his very own: **"Cribb "The Champion of England!"**

Cribb retired after the second Molineaux bout, but came out of retirement nine years later to fight and beat Jack Carter in 1820. He did spar several exhibitions throughout the years, but these were only when he was an honored guest during functions and were largely for effect.

Cribb was considered a national hero for the rest of his life. In retirement, he became a coal merchant and then ran a tavern called the Union Arms. By 1839, he had lost every penny he had and was forced to turn over the Union Arms to his creditors. Cribb moved in with his son, who was a baker, and his daughter-in-law. The tavern was eventually renamed the Tom Cribb Pub and is still in operation today. Cribb's health deteriorated and he died on May 11, 1848 at sixty-seven years old.

Tom Cribb was inducted into the International Boxing Hall of Fame in 1991 and was an inaugural inductee for the Bare Knuckle Hall of Fame in 2009. In addition to forever being labeled the Champion of England, Cribb is also credited for being the First World Champion based on his victories over Tom Molineaux, who had been recognized as the American Champion.

Chapter 8

After the second defeat to Cribb, Bill Richmond tried to get Molineaux to change his ways. He told Tom that the only reason he lost the fight was because he had abandoned his training and he had spent too much time drinking and womanizing. Molineaux would not listen. He continued to drink and hang with the ladies, although now, twice beaten by Cribb, some of the novelty was gone, which resulted in Tom spending more time with the lower class women and the prostitutes.

Richmond knew that Molineaux had the talent to make money in prizefighting, for both of them, but Tom would have to conform and listen to Richmond. Bill thought if he gave Tom some time, he might understand and change his ways. Molineaux showed no signs of reform. He had increased his drinking and was often causing trouble when drunk at Richmond's Horse and Dolphin. All Tom cared about was drinking and sleeping with the ladies and when he wasn't in a bed somewhere, he would publicly complain about Richmond. Molineaux felt that it was Richmond's fault that he lost the Cribb rematch. He would tell all that would listen that Bill had taken advantage of Molineaux.

One night in November of 1811, two months after the second Cribb match, Tom was drinking at the Horse & Dolphin and he became belligerent, as usual. Jack Power, who was at the Tavern and who was also a prizefighter, got into an argument with Molineaux, which quickly escalated. Before long, the two men took to the street, stripped and impromptu set-to. Tom was drunk and grossly out of shape and Power was a pugilist of note during the time. When the fight started, Power was able to land a few quick shots to the face of Molineaux, which caused Tom to wrestle Jack to the ground. When the two men got up, Tom's lip was bleeding. He furiously attacked Power, landing several hard shots to the head. Molineaux turned this brawl into a one-sided beat-down, as he was much bigger and more powerful than his adversary. Luckily for Jack Power, his friends intervened and broke up the fight after seventeen minutes. Power had taken a savage beating and it was quite possible that if his cohorts didn't stop the action, Molineaux very well could have beaten him to death. Tom returned to the tavern, drank some more and left with several vile women for the night.

Tom and Bill Richmond's relationship soon ended after Molineaux's street fight with Power outside the Horse and Dolphin. Even though Molineaux hadn't listened to Richmond since the first fight with Cribb, after the two parted ways, Tom fell deeper in his own degradation and self-abuse. He would scorn any advice given to him from his closest friends and would declare himself "an ill-used man." When he was intoxicated, he became mad and abusive towards himself as well as others. He would regularly engage in street fights and soon, was not welcome in most taverns throughout London.

For the next sixteen months, Tom traveled around the countryside putting on boxing exhibitions making enough money to keep him setup with booze and women. He was not concerned with eating properly, as his only interest in life was sex and alcohol.

On July 27, 1812, Molineaux tried his hand at wrestling at the Exeter Fair in London. He was paid to wrestle a man named John Snow. Because he was dreadfully out of shape, suffering from consumption and possibly from one or more sexually transmitted diseases, his performance was terrible. Snow dismantled the once seemingly invincible prizefighter, rather easily.

In 1813, a fighter named Bill Jay challenged Molineaux. On February 3, 1813 Jay had the following paragraph printed in the Leicester Paper:

"Jay, the pugilist, has challenged Molineaux to fight at any notice; but Blackee remains both deaf and dumb to this challenge, as he did to Crib's immediate acceptance of a vaunting challenge to him. The Champion promises him a love-dressing for his bounces, if he could be prevailed on to come to London."

Molineaux had his reply printed: "I, the said Molineaux, do declare, that I never received any challenge but through the medium of your print, but I am ready to fight him at any place, within the county of Leicester, for the sum not exceeding L200, if accepted within one month of the above date. In opposition to that part of the paragraph which relates to Cribb, I declare that I sent him a challenge, within two months, but I have receive no answer, my friends being mentioned in the challenge, who would back me to any amount; and that I have never received any challenge from Cribb, since I last fought him."

But the fight with Bill Jay or a third encounter with Cribb never materialized.

During the end of February 1813, Tom Molineaux had an offer to fight Jack Carter, who was trained, managed and backed by Bill Richmond. The fight was scheduled to take place on March 31, 1813 for one hundred guineas per side. But sometime prior to the fight date, Richmond had Molineaux arrested and thrown into jail for his un-paid debt, which was from the loan of the stake money for the second Cribb fight.

It's not known how much the debt was for, nor is it documented how the debt was satisfied, but by the first   week of April, Tom was released from jail and the debt was recorded as paid in full. What is known is that the friction between Richmond and Molineaux was at an all-time high. It had gotten to the point where each man wanted to hurt the other in any way possible. For Richmond, it was the public slander from Molineaux that had driven him to hate Tom. Molineaux blamed Bill for not training him properly and he'd tell everyone who'd listen at the pubs. Molineaux also felt that Bill used him as a cash cow and had made plenty of profit off of his sweat and blood. He also felt that Richmond forced Tom to take several additional rounds of punishment in the first Cribb encounter.

Richmond wanted the Molineaux-Carter fight. After working with his new young fighter, Bill thought that he was ready to beat Molineaux. When Tom Molineaux was released from jail, the fight with Jack Carter was rescheduled.

On April 23, 1813 at Remington, Gloucestershire, an out-of-shape Tom Molineaux was ready to set-to with Jack Carter. Or was he? Henry Miles described the two combatants: *"one was afraid and the other dared not."* This was a strange bout to say the least! As soon as the contest started, Tom Molineaux began acting afraid, running around the ring, yelling and screaming acting totally out of his mind. During each round, Molineaux made accusations to the referee that Carter was biting him and that his own seconds were out to get him. Molineaux was yelling as he was running around the ring, *"oh dear, oh dear...murder, murder!"* In between rounds, Molineaux had to be coaxed and coddled by his seconds into continuing to remain in the fight. Tom kept trying to leave the ring, but each time, he was calmed down enough to come out for the next stanza. Was Tom going mad? Everyone in attendance thought so! They all were perplexed to say the least. These strange actions by Molineaux went on for twenty-four rounds. There was virtually no action during this bout, except for Tom running around the ring screaming and Jack Carter chasing after him. At the end of the twenty-fourth round, Carter was sitting on Richmond's knee getting ready to come out for the twenty-fifth when all of a sudden; he fainted and as a result, could not continue. Tom Molineaux was awarded a twenty-five round victory.

Some believe that Jack Carter tired himself out by chasing Molineaux for twenty-four rounds and then collapsed due to fatigue, but most in attendance felt this was a set-up or fixed fight. The spectators booed the result and Tom Molineaux's name sank faster and further ill repute.

The odd encounter with Jack Carter was the last fight that Tom Molineaux would fight on English soil. The word of the strange bout spread quickly and soon, all of England and beyond had heard of the fiasco.

As if the match with Carter wasn't strange enough, soon after the bout was over, Tom Molineaux teamed up with J a c k Carter and both men set off to tour Scotland. The two would re-enact their now infamous battle to sold-out crowds throughout Scotland! The people of Scotland loved it and both Tom and Jack made out very well. After the shows, Tom would be found in the taverns and during the late evenings, would find himself in many different beds. His health was deteriorating very quickly.

During the tour, sometime during 1813, Molineaux and Carter found themselves in the town of Derby giving a boxing exhibition. A local man, Abraham Denston, who called himself a pugilist, challenged Tom Molineaux to a contest with gloves. Denston, who was a big man with Herculean strength, felt he could best Tom by overpowering him. He thought that by wearing the gloves, it would help him withstand the onslaught of Molineaux's boxing skill. All the locals were excited about the contest and most thought Denston would be a worthy opponent for Tom. Denston and his countrymen felt that his size alone would help him defeat Molineaux. Unfortunately for Abraham Denston, he had grossly miscalculated Tom's abilities. Tom Molineaux only needed two rallies to convince the Derby man he had had enough.

Egan describes the end of the fight: *"Molineaux punished the chaw-bacon most severely for his temerity, and with one of his favourite left-handed lunges, gave him such a remembrancer under his left eye, that the claret flew in all directions. The conceit of Abraham had now evaporated, and his quickly retired amidst the laughter and confusion of the audience, to disencumber himself of the gloves."*

Molineaux still had bad feelings for Richmond. Jack Carter also felt that Bill Richmond mistreated him too. Both Molineaux and Carter hoped that they would someday get a chance to get back at Richmond. But Richmond wasn't very fond of Molineaux or Carter either and unknown to the two touring fighters, Richmond had just arrived in Scotland with another young fighter he was training named, William Fuller.

William Fuller began his prizefighting career in 1812. Fuller was a clever fighter who showed promise and had great physical power, but just like Molineaux had been when he first came to Richmond, Fuller was extremely raw. When Fuller and Richmond met, he had just been beaten handily by Bill Jay, the same Bill Jay that had challenged Tom Molineaux several months earlier. Richmond refined Fuller's skills and taught him how to fight correctly. As a result, Richmond setup a rematch with Jay and in the second fight, William Fuller destroyed Bill Jay in forty-two minutes. After that, Richmond felt that Fuller was ready to fight and beat Tom Molineaux.

Bill Richmond knew that Molineaux was not the same fighter he was when he stepped in the ring with Cribb during their first encounter. When word got back to Molineaux that Richmond was in town with a new fighter, Tom felt that he could possibly get some measure of vengeance upon Richmond by beating his new young prospect. He didn't have to wait long because immediately after hearing of Richmond's presence in Scotland, William Fuller issued a challenge to Tom Molineaux. Despite not knowing anything about William Fuller, except that he was working with Richmond, Molineaux accepted the challenge. Both fighters put up one hundred guineas and the match was set.

Molineaux met William Fuller on May 27, 1814 at Bishopstorff, Peesley, Ayrshire, which was about twelve miles from Glasgow. Bill Richmond had instructed Fuller to demand a forty-foot ring. He knew that Molineaux was not in good shape and that Fuller, being younger and in peak condition, would have a distinct advantage if he forced Tom to chase him around the large ring. Molineaux, who was taking Fuller extremely lightly, agreed to the unusually large ring quickly. By daybreak on the morning of the contest, numerous vehicles of all sizes were making their way towards the site. There was a lot of interest in this fight as almost five thousand spectators were in attendance.

The two combatants met in the center of the ring. Tom Molineaux was seconded by only Carter, while William Fuller had George Cooper and Joe Ward working his corner. Bill Richmond chose to be a spectator for reasons unknown. Many who were in attendance and who had seen Tom Molineaux fight before noticed a complete change in Molineaux. He was not only a shell of himself in the ring in terms of his boxing ability, but his lifestyle had altered his appearance. This was not the same man that fought for the World Title in 1810.

The odds prior to the bout were set at five-to-four in favor of Molineaux to win the fight, five-to-two in favor of Molineaux to draw first blood and two-to-one that Tom would floor

Fuller first. Molineaux was so sure of victory that he bet every penny he had on himself to win all three.

Molineaux and Fuller shook hands and the contest began right around 1:00 pm. As the fight started, both men sparred, and as Egan noted, *"Both the combatants displayed good science."* Fuller was able to land several shots, but none seemed to have much pop behind them. Molineaux seemed to be headhunting, or he may have been conserving his limited energy and only threw a few punches, but he made them count, all landing with plenty of power. The two prizefighters seemed to be feeling each other out when the Sheriff of Renfrewshire, accompanied by several constables, entered the ring and put an end to the match. The fight had lasted only eight minutes.

Both fighters were not happy, especially Tom Molineaux who said, *"Had I anticipated such an interruption, I would have finished Fuller off before the arrival of the Sheriff!"*
Tom drew first blood and was able to collect on that bet, but neither of the other two bets was decided due to the interruption of the bout.

William Fuller wanted to continue the contest the very next day at another location, but Molineaux insisted on it to be the following Tuesday, which both ended up agreeing upon.

On Tuesday, May 31, 1814 Molineaux and Fuller met again, this time at Auchineaux on the Dryman road, which was less than fifteen miles from Glasgow. Again, Bill Richmond mysteriously sat with the spectators while Ward and Cooper seconded Fuller. An Irish Sergeant named Hailward and his private, whose name was not known, seconded Tom Molineaux. The umpires for this match were Captain Cadogan and George Stirling. The referee was a man from Guntmaux named Graham.

Pierce Eagan wrote: *"This battle is without parallel. There is nothing like it in the annals of pugilism."*

There was a lot of action during this fight. The fight lasted for only two rounds, but it took sixty-eight minutes! This was a brutal contest, which left both men battered beyond recognition.

Henry Miles wrote: *"Had Fuller been in the ring with the "Terrible Black" with whom Tom Cribb contended, and not a frail imposter, he would have been beaten down in less than fifteen minutes!"*

Excerpts from an actual ringside report were as follows: First round Fuller displayed some good positions, and soon convinced the spectators that he was a scientific boxer. His guard was firm and imposing, and he seemed confident of success. Molineaux did not view his opponent with indifference, but flattered himself that Fuller must ultimately be defeated. They sparred a considerable time, with good skill, before any punishment was exhibited, when Fuller, by a tremendous hit, drew the cork of his antagonist. The Black, upon the claret making its appearance, became rather impetuous, and attacked Fuller with great ferocity, but the latter stopped with much adroitness, and gave in exchange some heavy nobbing returns. A desperate rally now took place, during which severe milling was felt upon both sides, when they broke away, and again resorted to sparring to obtain superiority. Fuller's nose was much peppered, and the crimson flowed abundantly. In short this unprecedented round was filled up with rallies ~ recoveries ~ retreating ~ following each other alternately round the ring, ~ stopping and hitting with various success, ~ and both exhausted by turns, till at length Molineaux was leveled by a tremendous blow, and the round finished after a lapse of TWENTY-EIGHT MINUTES!

Second – To describe anything like the various changes which occurred during this set-to, it must partake more of the length of **"Patterson's Road Book,"** *than the ordinary round of a fight! But suffice to observe, that the whole minutiae of the milling art was restored to, from the beginning to the end. The skill, practice and experience of both the combatants were made use of to the best advantage. Fuller proved himself a boxer of more than ordinary science and game throughout the fight. The Black was convinced he had got a troublesome customer to deal with, and who required serving out in a masterly deficient from his former exhibitions, when he used to hit his men away from him, and leveled his opponents with the most perfect sang froid. The sever blows of Fuller, who stuck close to Molineaux, made him wince again! The Black appeared much exhausted from the great portion required for him to give, and heartily tired of what he had to take. An unusual quantity of blood was spilt. It is supposed Fuller lost two quarts in the ring. His head was terrific in the extreme. From the dreadful punishment his nob had undergone, his seconds lost all traces of his original character. Stauncher game was never displayed by any pugilist whatever. Upon the whole it was a truly singular fight, and the people of Scotland witnessed one of the most nouvelle specimens of English prize- fighting that ever occurred. In SIXTY-EIGHT MINUTES, two rounds only had taken place.*

As the second round was near its end, Molineaux was gasping for air and as a last ditch effort, unleashed a pulverizing right hand to the temple of Fuller that put him in serious trouble. The force of Molineaux's blow sent William Fuller staggering back toward his corner, as Tom followed him ready to land another shot that would have finished the game young fighter. But as Fuller fell back towards the ropes, and before Tom could land the final blow of the fight, Joe Ward, one of Fuller's seconds, pulled Fuller down to end the round.

Tom immediately appealed to the umpires. Molineaux claimed that Ward's move had interfered with his attack, which prevented Tom from finishing his opponent off. The umpires discussed the situation and soon decided that Molineaux was indeed correct. The actions of Fuller's corner were illegal, which meant the fight ended on a foul and the victory, and the purse, was awarded to Tom Molineaux. The official time was two rounds at sixty-eight minutes.

This fight proved beyond any doubt, that Tom Molineaux, like he had displayed previously during his earlier fights, could take a lot of punishment. But, unlike during the peak of his career, when he trained properly, he was unable to display his once unheralded offensive power and relentlessness.

Molineaux may not have been in much demand in England, but Scotland loved him! The Scots proved to be great hosts for Tom Molineaux. After his victory over William Fuller, he took his earnings and did what he loved to do best; he drank and whored around until he was broke once more.

Molineaux continued to tour Scotland and made enough money entertaining with boxing exhibitions to keep his belly full of booze and his evening bed occupied with women. Although the deterioration of his body continued, due to the consumption and sexually transmitted diseases, he still possessed enough skill to handle the toughs from town to town despite the clear fact he was a shell of his old self.

Tom, who once had a body Adonis would be jealous of, which was made of finely toned muscle, had now degenerated to fat and loose skin. His eyes were red and sunken and his skin had a yellowish tinge to it. He would often throw-up blood and his insides were ravaged by drink and disease. It was clear that Tom Molineaux was dying. Tom was no longer in any condition to fight for money, or in exhibitions.

Despite his failing health, on March 11, 1815 he fought George Cooper outside of Edinburgh. Tom Molineaux put in a lack luster performance to say the least. Molineaux was not able to defend himself and took a savage, one-sided, fourteen round beating from the younger prizefighter, which lasted twenty minutes before Cooper was declared the winner.

Molineaux was not the same fighter he was just five years earlier. As a matter of fact, he wasn't a fraction of the fighter he was even after his second bout with Cribb. The boxing exhibition tour of Scotland was over for Tom Molineaux and Jack Carter. They parted ways. Tom was not able to fight any level of fighter at this point. All he could do now was teach boxing, so he decided to move on, this time, to Ireland.

Chapter 9

Tom teamed up with his conqueror, George Cooper, and set out to tour Ireland where he had hoped he could make money teaching the art of boxing and giving boxing exhibitions. The two men arrived sometime during May of 1815 and were met with much curiosity. Cooper was still a quality fighter; but Molineaux was nothing but a shell of himself. The truth was Tom was not fit to fight. Not in a prizefight or in exhibition bouts but yet there was still much interest in him. Molineaux's reputation and his two battles with Cribb had been well publicized and his popularity was enough to still draw a crowd. But whether people wanted to see him as a prize-fighter or more as just a circus act was not known or documented.

The two men traveled through the smaller towns putting on boxing exhibitions. They drew decent-sized crowds and were earning some money, but nothing that was making them rich. Molineaux's habits were the same as they had been; as soon as there was money in his pocket, he spent it on booze and women, and Molineaux was not making enough to both feed his habits, and keep a roof over his head. However, there was a fighter in Ireland who just may have been able to give Molineaux the payday he needed to fix his finances. That fighter's name was Dan Donnelly.

Dan Donnelly was the Irish Champion and was considered a national hero. The people of Ireland loved him and he loved his country. He was a quality fighter and he too was seeking a big fight. Donnelly had just fought Jack Carter in April and had spent every penny he had earned from the contest. He was known as a bit of a playboy who liked to party. Donnelly was working as a carpenter trying to earn a little steady money

117

when he got word that two men were in town and they wanted to speak to him.

It was June of 1815 when Tom Molineaux and George Cooper sat in a local tavern waiting to speak with Dan Donnelly. When Donnelly arrived, he went straight to the bar, ordered a drink and waited for the two strangers to come to him, and before long, Molineaux and Cooper did.

"Sir, I perceive you are Mr. Dan Donnelly," said Tom Molineaux. Donnelly acknowledged that he was indeed and so Molineaux continued, *"This is George Cooper and I am Tom Molineaux. We are in Ireland on an exhibition tour and to teach boxing. We have been told that you are the best fighter in Ireland and I would like to challenge you to a match."*

Donnelly did not respond at first. Instead, he took a sip of his drink. Several minutes went by until he spoke, *"No, I do not wish to fight a conquered man, nor would I fight a colored man"* Donnelly said, looking them both up and down. *"But I am willing to fight Mr. Cooper if he so desires."*

Molineaux became enraged at the curt response and dismissal by the Irish Champion and began to insult Donnelly, wanting to fight him right then and there. Cooper had to hold Tom back from attacking Donnelly. After some coaxing, George Cooper calmed Molineaux down and then turned to Donnelly smiling, and said that he would be happy to fight him. The two men shook hands and agreed upon a bout, as Molineaux looked on astonished.

Dan Donnelly and George Cooper met on December 13, 1815 in what turned out to be one of the most famous battles in Irish boxing history and is still celebrated today, with re- enactments. Even the location of the fight is named Donnelly's Hollow to this day and the Irish   Champion's footprints to the location of the ring are carved out and preserved. His victory that day was well celebrated, then and now. Donnelly died suddenly at the age of thirty-two. Even after his death, he continued to make news, as his body was stolen from its grave, only to be returned, less one arm, which is still in circulation today. It was most recently part of the Fighting Irishmen Exhibition at the GAA Museum, Croke Park in Dublin during 2010. Dan Donnelly was inducted into the International Boxing Hall of Fame in 2008.

As if being insulted by Dan Donnelly was not enough, his own touring partner, George Cooper as a matter of factly, stabbed Molineaux in the back by accepting Donnelly's challenge right in front of Tom Molineaux. Tom was furious and stormed out of the tavern never to see or speak to George Cooper again.

Molineaux was all but lost, mentally and physically. He no longer had a sparring partner to perform in boxing exhibitions, nor did he have any desire to find one. He had felt the world deserted him and that everyone who he thought was his friend betrayed him. All he was able to do now was travel from town to town and teach boxing for whatever money he could get. He managed to survive for the next two years living day by day.

Molineaux's health was declining very rapidly. His alcohol abuse worsened and complications from consumption and the sexually transmitted diseases continued to ravish his once Herculean body. By the beginning of 1818, his skin was almost yellow and his eyes had become sunken to the point of where he began to resemble a living skeleton. Molineaux became weaker by the day and soon, he was not able to teach boxing and was forced to live on handouts.

By the summer of 1818, Molineaux was in Galway and his condition got to the point where he was no longer able to care for himself. He was forced to rely on others to keep food in his stomach, clothes on his back and a roof over his head. He had to rely on others to keep him alive. This once seemingly invincible man had become helpless.

By the middle of July of 1818 he had become close with three black American solders that were members of the 77th Regiment Foot Band, who were stationed in Galway. The three black solders cared for the first American Heavyweight Champion, by feeding, bathing and comforting him. Molineaux was provided a warm place to sleep inside a storage closet where the Foot Band's equipment was kept.

Tom died on August 4, 1818 when his body shut down. He was found in the storage closet. He was thirty-four years old. At the time of his death, he was penniless, his body was reduced to a skeleton with skin that weighed less than eighty pounds and he had been unable to walk, eat or drink.

Tom had died alone, just as he had set out for England only nine years earlier.

The exact location of Molineaux's grave is considered unknown, however *The Galway Advertiser* reported on February 10, 1994 that archaeologist Jim Higgins had claimed to have "made some spectacular discoveries at the St. James Church in Ballybane" where conservation work had been going on at its ruined building. According to the article, the Joyce's, of Merview House and the Wilson-Lynch family of Renmore House, had apparently used the grounds for their family tombs. The article goes on to say that "among those buried there was Tom Molineaux."

On April 21, 2010, The *Irish Times* reported that several students from Galway Community College had been involved with a project exploring the life & times of Tom Molineaux. One of the students, Sheona Joyce said, "We took a trip to the

Renmore Army barracks and the Merview graveyard where Molineaux is believed to have been buried after he died, but sadly we couldn't find his grave, but we left flowers by the gate in his honor."

Merview House is in the town of Ballybaunbeg, which is about a mile northeast of Galway city. The fact that it's believed that Tom Molineaux is buried in an unknown, unmarked grave seems to follow the treatment this man endured during his life and times, despite his one-time world-wide fame and his accomplishments.

How sadder can an ending be?

Afterword

One of the hardest parts during the research on Tom Molineaux's life was the poor record keeping during his lifetime in the United States. To make it even harder, he was a black man during a time when most people didn't consider him an equal because of Slavery.

During my research, I found an essay written by Lindsey Williams in the early 1980's who claimed that George Washington introduced Tom Molineaux to Prize Fighting during the final years of his life. I was able to contact and speak with Mr. Williams and he referred me to a book that was written in 1810 about George Washington. I did not find anything in that book that mentioned Williams claim.

Author Bill Paxton forwarded me an article that also mentioned that George Washington was at one time the Virginia Amateur Bare-Knuckle Boxing Champion as a sixteen-year-old teenager, but again I could not make a connection to Tom Molineaux.

However, when I created a timeline, it IS very possible that during the last four years of George Washington's life, he could have influenced Tom Molineaux.

I based this book only on fact, so I did not include giving George Washington any credit for Tom Molineaux's accomplishments, but it was possible that they did meet, but to what degree, I can't back up with fact. From what I found, Molineaux learned how to box from his Father and the rest from his own experiences and technique he learned from Bill Richmond.

I believe that Tom Molineaux is a very important part of American History as well as boxing history. He was a man that won his freedom in the prizefighting ring and traveled around the world without any friends or money. This was a special person. He had no formal education, but yet he accomplished more than most ever dreamed of during his time and even today. I feel strongly about how he was treated in England. He was blatantly robbed of the World Title, but to me, it goes much deeper than that one fight. The fact that he is virtually a forgotten man is even more of a travesty than his experiences inside the ring.

The International Boxing Hall of Fame and the Bare Knuckle Boxing Hall of Fame both recognize Tom Hyer as the First American Champion in 1849. They also recognize George Godfrey as the First black American Champion in 1879.

Tom Molineaux left the United States as The American Heavyweight Champion in 1809. That would make him not only the first black American Champion seventy years prior to Godfrey, but that would make him the FIRST AMERICAN CHAMPION FORTY years prior to Hyer!

Consider this; Tom Cribb is the first English Champion to fight for the World Title. That contest was the one that they robbed victory from Molineaux in December of 1810. How could Cribb be fighting for a World Title IF Molineaux did not possess the Title of American Champion? If Molineaux was not the American Heavyweight Champion, the fight(s) with Cribb would have been for the English Heavyweight Championship. It's pretty simple if you give it any thought.

I think it's time we correct history and give Tom Molineaux the credit he deserves. Unfortunately, we can't correct the wrong that was done during his fight, nor can we correct the wrongs done during his lifetime, but we CAN correct the way we recognize our boxing history that took place in the   United

States. If the American History books don't want to give credit where credit is due, then it's up to Boxing History to do so. No matter how you look at it, a CORRECTION must be made.

Molineaux was the very first American Heavyweight Champion in 1809. It doesn't matter what the color of his skin was. It doesn't matter that he was born into slavery as a slave. What does matter is that he was an American and he was the first American Heavyweight Champion. I think it has been long enough. It's time we give him the credit he deserves. I think all Americans, and the future generations of Americans need to get it right; they need to learn it the way it is and the way it happened. Tom Molineaux fought his way out of Slavery, became a free man; a free American became the first American Heavyweight Champion and was the first American to challenge for the World Heavyweight title. History can't be told in another other way.

Bill Calogero

Epilogue
By Daxx Khan

Tom Molineaux's journey through life was nothing short of remarkable! It started with his father Zachary who was a slave and fought during the revolutionary war. Considered a hero his reward for helping men break free from a nation who's King they considered a "Tyrant," Zachary was returned to slavery. So when Tom was born on the Molineaux Virginia plantation there were no aspirations for his future. Aspirations of a better life were for free men, not slaves. His fate seemed predetermined, from his success to demise.

As a slave its rumored Tom was treated kindly, but no matter how kindly a slave's life could be it was an unhappy miserable existence. Losing his father at the age of fourteen must certainly have added to that burden. Even the most uneducated man or woman born into slavery eventually realizes there is no brighter future ahead and only those you serve benefit from your existence. You are someone's "Property" and can easily be replaced.

I can only assume that with Algernon Molineaux making Tom a constant companion provided him slight advantages. An occasional day's break from hard labor, if they traveled off the plantation together, maybe a even bath and decent clothes for the day. I could hardly imagine someone of Algernon's wealthy status, willing to be accompanied by a slave who was dingy from working on his plantation.

As a boy in his mid-teens, without a father to guide him, any favoritism shown by Algernon could very well have been misleading to Tom. It's possible Tom may have even confused Algernon using him as a companion for friendship. Should that have been the case when Tom learned he was thrust into a bout against Abe, it must have stung him to the bone!

There is little doubt in my mind that Abe had a fierce reputation. Word of men such as Abe spread quickly and I am sure the word had passed by Tom's ears. Reputations like Abe's often instill fear in men, let alone a seventeen year old boy.

Unless Abe had already proven himself against other men, why else would Randolph Peyton have bragged about Abe? Even if Peyton may have been a bit intoxicated from drinking at the party, or antagonizing Algernon it was an enormous sum of money to bet.

That fear added with anger that Algernon had put him in such a situation, might have been why Tom gave little effort in his training at first. Hoping if he showed little promise the bout would be called off. Algernon beating Tom, an already scared seventeen year old with nothing to gain, unquestionably did more damage towards his own cause than good. Slave or not most teenagers filled with anger and hurt, even today, would rather suffer than help who caused it.

When physical pain subsides it's all but forgotten; Algernon beating Tom might have brought out rebellion. Tom's form of rebellion was possibly refusing to dedicate himself completely towards learning the teachings of Patrick Davis.

However, a reward in most cases is motivation for anyone and certainly more effective than a beating. Ask any parent who has raised a teenager, what methods more effective in getting them to maximize their potential. The threat of being grounded for a month or borrowing the car for a night? I could almost guarantee the latter has always worked more effectively. Imagine the motivation that promises of freedom and money would bring out of a teenage boy living a life of slavery. Algernon was smart in taking Patrick Davis' advice. Only Tom Molineaux knows what went through his mind the night he took on Randolph Peyton's best man Abe. More than likely it was a combination of both fear and idea he could be a free man. Together along with Patrick Davis' training Tom was victorious over Abe and now free.

Fighters are born not made and that night in 1801 the fighter born inside Tom Molineaux emerged. Yet it was only the start of his journey.

His arrival in New York I believe may have been the most difficult time of Tom's life. New York City has always possessed a bustling atmosphere filled with elements of all sorts. Even today, for those unfamiliar with life in the big city, it can be overwhelming. At least on the Molineaux plantation Tom knew when he would eat, where he would lay his head at night and what was expected of him.

With no understanding on how the world works, Tom was now stepping into the "Unknown." Where would he lay his head? How would he put food in his stomach? Where would he be accepted?

When Tom ended up at the Catherine Street Market, he saw a potential to earn money and noticed very few cared about his skin color. Initially he was more than likely excited and thrilled to have a place he fit in. Even if it was not the most desirable place at least he was as a free man and was able to make his own decisions.

Turning to prizefighting surely seemed a smart idea, until learning how brutal the bouts could be. Then after understanding if he was hurt during a bout and he could be left for dead somewhere, his decision might have been a bit regretted. Having little to no other options, he was in a desperate situation. Fortunately the "Fighter" in Tom had already emerged when he beat Abe to a pulp. So he proceeded to do what fighters do; bring "A means to an end" using his fists.

In the mid 1980's a troubled young kid, by the name of Mike Tyson burst onto the boxing scene. Tyson was younger than Tom was when he had arrived in New York City. Prior to boxing Mike also had few options in life, until Cus D'Amato would take charge of him.

Tom Molineaux and Mike Tyson's life would both take similar paths over the years despite being almost 200 years apart. Cus taught Mike the sport of boxing, what he could become if he dedicated himself and worked hard and dug deep. Tom never quite had the type mentor Cus was to Tyson, but he learned the success and luxuries in life Prizefighting could bring. He would also experience the heartache of what it was when those around you put their best interest first.

After Cus passed away Mike was left to figure things out on his own before his 21st birthday. Trust was a huge issue for Mike as was fear. Like Tom, that night on the Molineaux plantation, Mike had become a "Fighter" in the Catskill gym. It would be boxing that created their legacy and place in history.

Tyson many times self admittedly would walk towards the ring filled with fear but he would turn that fear into fuel. That fuel turned him into a winner. The more victories he piled up, the more self-confident he became and eventually a World Champion. Tom Molineaux turned his fear of the unknown into fuel. As it did for Tyson, that fuel turned him into a winner and eventually a champion.

Tyson and Molineaux both quickly took a liking to their new found celebrity status. Prior to prize fighting nobody knew who they were, having people know them by sight was a pleasant new experience. So was having more money than either ever imagined. They both also spent their money just as quickly.

Prizefighters have always had a bad habit of spending their money fast and recklessly. They come to believe more is only a fight away. While active and successful that may hold true. They fail to plan out what they will do when no more paydays are left. Hundreds of fighters who have become champions made that same mistake, sometimes more than once.

Mike Tyson, despite his incredible success, wasted his prime in and out of trouble with the law. Alcohol and women were other vices that hurt his early career. Molineaux would also drink and spend too much time with loose women and nothing good came from his recklessness either.

Each man would maintain drawing power up until their final bout and both walked away in an embarrassing fashion. Horribly out of shape they were dominated by opponents once not worthy of sharing the same ring.

The signs that Tom was in steady decline and his time short was the Jack Carter bout. Molineaux running around in an almost demented state against Jack is almost impossible to imagine. The closest thing I could compare it to from the description provided by newspapers of the time is Oliver McCall's mental breakdown in his rematch against Lennox Lewis. McCall started to cry uncontrollably which forced referee Mills Lane to halt the contest. Molineaux actually wore Carter out by forcing Jack to chase Tom around the ring trying to land effective punches. Eventually, Molineaux earned a victory when Carter could chase him no longer due to exhaustion.

Tom's last hurrah was the tour of exhibitions with George Cooper, the same type of exhibitions Tyson would conduct with former heavyweight prospect Cory Sanders. They were so out of shape neither could even put on a decent show for those who paid money. That's how far their skills had declined.

When Tyson had no choices left and his ability to earn a living inside the ring had past, his celebrity status carried him after boxing. He has become one of the most loved champions of all time despite the chaos in his life, before, during and after boxing. If only Molineaux had been so lucky.

Like Jerry Quarry, the 1970's heavyweight contender, oddly enough was of Irish descent, a country Molineaux spent his last days. Neither could care for themselves in the end suffering with only memories of what once was and could have been. They were sympathetic figures for those who cared for them. Yet each man is hardly mentioned and all but forgotten today.

Tom heading to England after no more challenges in America were available seemed like a logical choice. What a blow to Tom's ego it must have been when he realized he was literally an unknown fighter.

As a twenty five year old young man with an ego who held the title of "American Champion," his mind must have wondered, "How could this be?"

In today's era with the Internet and television, Tom would have arrived from America with a huge amount of anticipation from the fans. When he started telling everyone "I am champion of America" and seeking out Tom Cribb, Molineaux unknowingly became his own promoter and PR man. It was a concept way ahead of its time.

His mission to fight Cribb was the era's comparison to a twenty two year old Cassius Clay seeking out Sonny Liston, telling everyone and anyone willing or not willing to listen "I am the greatest." I'm sure if there were television cameras available for Tom he might have come up with a poem or two and even drove around with Cribb on the side of a bus. Tom claiming he could beat any man was his way of stating "I am the greatest." At least people knew who Cassius Clay was; as an Olympic gold medalist who had televised wins over well know fighters.

Tom Molineaux claimed to be the American Champion, but it was just that; his claim nothing more. Even if he had some sort of title to show off no one had ever actually seen him fight. Clay and Molineaux knew how to draw attention, maybe not quite the attention he was looking for, but effective no less. Clay who later became Muhammad Ali had financial backers. Tom Molineaux needed to seek his own help in securing any fight, let alone a title fight. Opening doors of opportunity became a whole new obstacle for Molineaux.

Tom had no idea how the "Business" portion of the sport worked in the more organized London boxing scene. The word "Prize Fighting" means exactly what it implies and that prize (the money) had to be spread around.
Then as it is today unless the potential for profit is evident managers and trainers would rather invest their time elsewhere. You would be hard pressed to find a manager or promoter willing to take a chance investing in a fighter that might not show a return.

After being rejected by Bob Gregson, hooking up with Bill Richmond was the perfect opportunity for Tom. A former American slave with connections, one who had already fought Tom Cribb; the same man Tom was chasing. How could he go wrong?

At first Richmond seemed like the light at the end of Tom's tunnel. He knew how to make the best out of a fighter's natural ability; refine them and build up their reputation. His approach was an educated one as well. The sparring session against Cribb's manager, Robert Barclay, the fight against Jack Burrows, a Cribb protégé and Blake the sailor were with no question carefully thought out.

Richmond knew if the right people started to demand the fight between Molineaux and Cribb it would happen. He also knew the right people behind it would generate the most money. That plan worked out perfect when Lord Sackville became sold on Molineaux. Yet for all the good he did for Tom, once the fight was a done deal he failed him even more.

Richmond built Tom into a superstar, parading him off like a sideshow with the press and public watching his every move. There's no doubt in my mind that Bill Richmond loved every minute of the spotlight.

As he watched Tom develop bad habits, he failed to truly assert himself by making sure Tom stayed focused. Bill Richmond was well aware Tom's lifestyle would bring him down before any opponent, yet he wasn't going to deter Tom from having a good time. That would possibly risk Molineaux, who had become Richmond's meal ticket, taking a walk. In a sense, but not setting Molineaux straight, Richmond helped in the swelling of Tom's head from the attention. Richmond was more of a "Cheerleader" at this point rather than a trainer and advisor. It was obvious that in Tom's mind he was already the champion. There was no reason for him to train hard; those around him enforced his opinion.

Richmond also knew as Cribb read reports Molineaux was living it up instead of training, he would work harder at getting prepared. Attention and money still remained his primary focus.

Like Algernon Molineaux so many years before, Richmond needed Tom for his own benefit. Everything else was an afterthought.

I guess you could say Richmond was looking to "Cash Out" on Molineaux in the Cribb fight. If that had not become his intentions there would have been some effort made to stop Tom's out of control lifestyle.

It all started to backfire on Richmond, just when he needed Tom to focus. The realization of what he had created set in and Richmond started to see everything starting to fly away. Then Tom started training seriously.

The fight itself was what every great fight to follow was and more combined. There was Arturo Gatti vs. Micky Ward back and forth action where no one gained full control for an extended period. Each man was down more times than Primo Carnera was against Max Bear. As the rounds went on, both fighters showed astonishing recuperative abilities and the level of violence would have killed most men.

There was even the dreaded "Long Count." Like Dempsey did against Tunney in 1927 and Tyson against Douglas in 1990. Dempsey and Tyson lost their titles because of "Long Count's" Molineaux too had the chance to become champion.

Molineaux eventually collapsed from exhaustion, but what if he had not been in the taverns and carousing with women? Looking back on the punishment Cribb took and the fact he was almost out several times while Molineaux was still fresh, I firmly believe the chaotic camp leading up to the bout is what cost him in the end.

While we heard second hand accounts of how brutal the fight was, for any fight fan just imagining it gives an adrenaline rush.

Who is to blame though? Molineaux for not knowing better or Richmond for not looking after his fighter? Molineaux was a grown man responsible for his decisions but when Richmond took the role as his trainer and advisor it was his job to protect Tom, even if it was from himself.

Tom was never the same and he was never able to break his bad habits. After the Cribb rematch when Tom was easily beaten, Bill still believed in him, even after the Jack Carter debacle. Molineaux was still somewhat of a draw and could be profited off of. Richmond had some bad habits of his own because later on after the Molineaux vs. Jack Carter, Tom claimed Richmond had screwed him.

Like a true second rate promoter Richmond blamed both men for his wrong doings. In 200 years nothing has changed in that aspect of the sport. It continues; the matter of "Finger Pointing" when things go wrong. We only find out the truth after both have walked away from the sport.

Tom Molineaux's story is one that continues today, it continues to replay itself and only the lead characters change.

Jack Johnson had many of the same habits as Tom; drinking, womanizing and living the fast life. Even to the day of his own death, which was caused by traveling high speeds in his car, he lived life to its extreme.

Sugar Ray Robinson who may be the sports all-time greatest pound for pound fighter, craved attention and traveled with large entourages. He too ended up broke and suffering from Alzheimer's disease. Even the sports best ever ended up with nothing left to show for his years inside the ring.

Joe Frazier, who also had lived life so extravagantly, ended up broke living in hospice.   Like Molineaux and   Robinson,

"Smokin'" Joe had to be cared for by others suffering from the pain of liver cancer when he passed.

We claim to love these fighters for all they did inside the ring but when it's over we leave them alone as if they never existed. Still to this day, the only thing we give them is a few words of condolences and moment of pity.

Like Zachary Molineaux who was rewarded for fighting in the revolutionary war by being returned to slavery, we reward our fighters by allowing them to end up where they began; with nothing to show for everything they gave us.

Tom Molineaux was America's "First Champion;" he won that title fighting brutal bouts in the back rooms of New York City pubs and alleys. Over a century later Madison Square Garden would be built. Eventually without a single reference to him became it "The Mecca of Boxing" It's almost a cruel joke of a destiny that began with the blood off Tom's back.

Boxing's importance and history extends far beyond the ring. The hopes of millions have rested on one fighter's victory. Money generated through prize fighting at times has created such epic proportions of corruption and greed; laws were enacted to deter future offenders. Larger than life champions have been role models for fatherless boys they never met, who might have otherwise taken the wrong path in life.

The potential of money and fame has gravitated men of all ages towards boxing now for centuries. A chance at being admired by thousands or even millions while escaping poverty is a hard opportunity to pass by. Countless of would be fighters willing to give or risk taking a beating against an unknown opponent have seen it as their "Means to an End."

Start to finish is hard no matter how successful they become for a fighter and his career. The years of constant training, recovering from nagging or serious injuries and maintaining weight can be a daily struggle. Trying to balance a career and private life away from the sport while active can be overwhelming. It's something many have found impossible to balance.

Meanwhile we sit watching from the outside. We form opinions of fighters based on beatings they take or deliver inside the ring and judge them afterwards. We judge their performance and how much of themselves they were willing to sacrifice. Then we take it upon ourselves to decide if they could have done better. As observers we judge them unfairly yet believe it's our right. Maybe it's the measly price of admission we pay that makes us feel entitled? Perhaps because of their larger than life personas we place unreasonable expectations upon them. When realizing this, could we be judging a fighter's performance and their careers are a way of removing blame from ourselves? A refusal to admit it was ourselves who set the men we look up to for failure in no one's eyes but our own. I have no right answer why we feel the need to judge fighters. I can't even answer why I am guilty of doing it myself.

Once a fighter takes his gloves off for the last time and their final career bell rings we owe them. We may not be able to give back the parts of themselves they left behind but we can reserve their rightful place in history. A place they earned through the blood and sweat we watched them shed. Even if it's done so with the unfair judgment we take upon ourselves.

When a fighter is not given their deserved place in history we rob them of everything they worked so hard to accomplish as it seems to get erased. We rob their successors of an ability to learn from mistakes they are most likely to repeat. We rob ourselves of being able to appreciate their struggles and maybe think before judging so harshly.

Tom Molineaux's story when told before was omitted of crucial facts surrounding his success, while his failures embellished. Those embellishments often lead to that unfair judgment we tend to make.

One man did it before everyone and now, with nothing embellished or omitted his story has been told in full. A man who found a "Means to an end" though boxing.

A once docile slave who literally went from "Bondage to the Baddest Man on the Planet!" Let's just hope the name Tom Molineaux never gets lost again, or we will just continue robbing him and ourselves.

Daxx Khan – 2015
Boxing Writer & Radio Personality

Tom Molineaux Recorded Boxing Record
Total Recorded Record:
8 Wins – 4 Losses – 1 NC

Aliases: the "Virginia Slave," the "Moor," the "Black," the "New Black"

Born: 1784 on a Plantation in Virginia
Died: August 4, 1818 in Galway, Ireland

Height: 5' 9 ½"
Weight: 190-200lbs

Manager: Bill Richmond

Tom Molineaux was inducted into the International Boxing Hall of Fame in 1997 and was inducted into the Bare Knuckle Boxing Hall of Fame in 2010.

1801   Tom fought a Slave from a neighboring plantation named Abe. It lasted five rounds (no time is known) and Tom won by KO. He also won his freedom and left Virginia, the only place he had ever known, by himself, with only the earnings from the fight and the clothes on his back. (Win)

1804   No fights were recorded up to this point however; Tom was now in New York making a living as a Prize-Fighter.

1804-1809   Tom fought what is documented as "many fights" during this period in New York, although no opponents and results can be found. It has been said the Molineaux won all of his fights, except one, but was able to avenge that loss. By the end of 1808, Tom was considered the Heavyweight Champion of America. He arrived in England during the winter of 1809 penniless, friendless and alone, however, he did have his title of Heavyweight Champion of America.

July 24, 1810   Tothill Fields in Westminster, England
                       vs. Jack Burrows (Win)

August 21, 1810   Castle Tavern, England vs. Tom
                       "Tough" Blake (Win)

December 18, 1810   Copthall Common, England vs. Tom
                       Cribb for the World Heavyweight Title
                       (Loss)

May 21, 1811   Mousley Hurst, England vs. Rimmer
                       (Win)

September 28, 1811   Thistleton Gap, England vs. Tom Cribb
                       for the World Heavyweight Title
                       (Loss)

November 1811   Horse & Dolphin Tavern, England vs.
                       Jack Power (Win)

July 27, 1812   Exeter Fair in London, England vs.
                       John Snow (Loss)

April 23, 1813   Remington Gloucestershire, England vs.
                       Jack Carter (Win)

1813	Derby, Scotland vs. Abraham Denston (Win)
May 27, 1814	Scotland (12 miles from Glasgow) vs. William Fuller (NC)
May 31, 1814	Paisley, Scotland vs. William Fuller (Win)
March 11, 1815	Edinburgh, Scotland vs. George Cooper (Loss)

Bibliography

Pierce Egan, *Boxiana Vol. I* - Smeeton 1813

Pierce Egan, *Boxiana Vol. II* - Sherwood, Neely & Jones 1818

Pierce Egan, *Boxiana Vol. III* - Sherwood, Neely & Jones 1821

Henry Miles, *Pugilistica, Vol. I* – Weldon & Co., 1880

Richard K. Fox, *Prize Ring Champions of England from 1719 to 1889* – 1889

Richard K. Fox, *The Black Champions of the Prize Ring* – 1890

Editor of Bell's Life in London, *Fights For The Championship and Celebrated Prize Battles* - 1855

J.B. McCormick, *The Square Circle: Stories Of The Prize Ring* – Continental Publishing Company 1897

Nat Fleischer, *Black Dynamite, Vol. I* - The Ring Athletic Library 1938

Kevin Smith, *Black Genesis: The History Of The Black Prizefighter 1760-1870* – iUniverse, Inc. 2003

Mike Glenn, *The Integration Of Sports History: The Mike Glenn Collection*, Volume 2 - 2005

Jon Hurley, *Tom Cribb – The Life of the Black Diamond* – The History Press 2009

Patrick Myler, *Dan Donnelly 1788 – 1820* – The Lilliput Press 2010

Frederick Douglas, *Narrative of the life of Frederick Douglas, an American Slave* – Anti-Slavery Office #25 Cornhill, 1845

John Durant & Otto Bettmann, *Pictorial History of American Sports from Colonial Times to the Present* – 1952

Fred Henning, *Fights for the Championship; The Men and Their Times* – 1899

New York Clipper Newspaper from January 19, 1884

The National Police Gazette, London from September 28, 1898

Elliott J. Gorn, *The Manly Art: Bare-Knuckle Prize Fighting in America* – Cornwall Press 1986

International Boxing Hall of Fame's website: www.ibhof.com under the Enshrinee information for Tom Molineaux.

Information on "The Bristol" is located at: www.rhiw.com/y_mor/shipwrecks/the_bristol.htm